About the Author

Samir Amin was born in Egypt in 1931 an~~~ education in Paris in the fields of politics, statistics ~~~ the past 30 years he has established a worldwide ~~~ of the foremost radical thinkers of our generation on ~~~sing out of the changing nature of capitalism, North-South relations, and development theory. Among his many institutional roles, he has been Director of IDEP, the UN African Institute for Planning, and he currently heads the Third World Forum in Dakar, Senegal.

He is the author of numerous books in French and Arabic. Many of them have been translated into numerous other languages, including a dozen or more into English, notably by the Monthly Review Press in the United States and Zed Books in Britain. Perhaps his most famous works are *Accumulation on a World Scale* (1974) and *Unequal Development*. His most recent books in English are *Re-reading the Post-War World: An Intellectual Itinerary* (1994) and *Empire of Chaos* (1993).

His previous titles published by Zed Books:
The Arab Nation: Nationalism and Class Struggle (1978)
The Arab Economy Today (1992)
Eurocentrism (1989)
Maldevelopment: Anatomy of a Global Failure (1990)
Delinking: Towards a Polycentric World (1990)

Samir Amin

CAPITALISM IN THE AGE OF GLOBALIZATION

The Management of Contemporary Society

IPSR

Cape Town

ZED BOOKS

London & New York

Capitalism in the Age of Globalization was first published in 1997 by Zed Books Ltd, 7 Cynthia Street, London N1 9JF, UK and Room 400, 175 Fifth Avenue, New York, NY 10010, USA.

Distributed in the USA exclusively by St. Martin's Press, Room 400, 175 Fifth Avenue, New York, NY 10010, USA

Second impression, 1998
Third impression, 2000

Published in South Africa by the Institute for Policy and Social Research (IPSR), 41 Salt River Road, Salt River 7925, Cape Town in 1998

Published in Kenya by Friends of the Book Foundation, P.O. Box 39624, Nairobi

Copyright © Samir Amin, 1997

Typeset by Photosetting and Secretarial Services, Yeovil, Somerset
Printed and bound in the United Kingdom by Biddles Ltd, www.biddles.co.uk

Library of Congress Cataloging-in-Publication Data

Amin, Samir.
    Capitalism in the age of Globalization: the management of contemporary society / Samir Amin.
    p.   cm.
Includes bibliographical references and index.
ISBN 1-85649-467-5. — ISBN 1-85649-468-3 (pbk.)
1. Capitalism. 2. Business Cycles. 3. Competition.
International. I. Title
HB501.A5866 1996
330.12′2–dc20   96-34226
                                           CIP

Grateful acknowledgement is made for permission to reprint **Chapter 2,** originally published as 'Fifty Years is Enough', in *Monthly Review,* April 1995; **Chapter 3,** originally published as 'Replacing the International Monetary System?' in *Monthly Review,* October 1993; and **Chapter 7,** originally published in *African Development.*

Introduction and Chapter 6 are translated by Patrick Camiller. Chaper 1 is translated by Beatrice Wallerstein.

ISBN 1 85649-467 5 (Hb)
ISBN 1 85649 468 3 (Pb)

South African ISBN 0-9584224-2-7 (Hb)
South African ISBN 0-9584224-1-9 (Pb)

Contents

Acronyms

CODESRIA	Council for the Development of Social Research in Africa.
EBRD	European Bank for Recovery and Development.
ECLA	Economic Commission on Latin America.
EU-ACP	The Association of the European Union with Africa, the Caribbean and Pacific.
G7	Group of Seven.
GATT-WTO	General Agreement on Trade and Tariffs - World Trade Organisation.
ICVA	International Committee for Voluntary Agencies.
NAFTA	North American Free Trade Association.
NIEO	New International Economic Order.
OECD	Organisation of Economic Cooperation and Development.
TRIM	Trade Related Investment Measures.
TRIP	Trade Rights in Intellectual Property.
UNCTAD	UN Conference for Trade and Development.
UNDP	UN Development Programme.

Introduction

This work brings together seven studies of the capitalist management of the crisis in which humanity now, so obviously, finds itself.

Chapter 1 offers an analysis of the new forms of polarization induced by the gigantic changes brought about by the 'growth decades' (the 1950s and 1960s) that shaped a world system very different from that of the past. Globalization of the productive system means that the various countries now need to be classified according to the relative weight of the 'active army' and the 'reserve army' of labour within their society, these concepts being defined, in keeping with the logic of globalization, by reference to the segments of the productive system that are more or less competitive at a world level. Using this criterion, the great bulk of labour power in the heartlands (i.e. the centre) participates in the active army, because of the way in which central economies gradually took shape in favourable conditions that cannot be repeated today. In the peripheral industrialized countries of Latin America, East Asia (communist and capitalist) and the ex-Soviet world, segments of the productive system are already (or may become) competitive in the above sense. The active army of labour exists here and may continue its progression. But it will never, as far into the future as we can see, be able to absorb the reserve from the rural and informal economies – both because global competitiveness now requires techniques of production that make such absorption impossible, and because the safety-valve of mass emigration is not available. As for the non-industrial and/or non-competitive peripheral countries of Africa and the Arab world, the situation is still more dramatic: the active army barely exists at all, virtually the whole nation being a reserve in world terms.

Third World industrialization will not, therefore, put an end to the polarization inherent in actually existing world capitalism. But it will move the forms and mechanisms to other planes, where they will be governed by the centre's financial, technological, cultural and military monopolies through which the new form of the globalized law of value produces polarization. What is more, such industrialization will not reproduce social evolution in the image of the developed West. The welfare state, and the capital/labour compromise it implies, came about after society had already been transformed through a long process. In this preparatory phase, large-scale mechanized industry was supported by a permanent agricultural revolution, while emigration to the Americas offered an outlet for the pressures of Europe's population explosion, and colonial conquest brought in supplies of cheap raw materials. Thus, when the welfare state appeared, it reinforced a historic compromise between capital and labour made easier by the reduction in the reserve army within the countries of the centre. The industrializing Third World, on the other hand, had none of these favourable conditions that might have averted the wilder forms of capitalist expansion. And in what one may call the Fourth World, excluded from industrialization at that time, the social system has thrown up extremes bordering on caricature; the reserve army here comprises the great majority of the population – the marginalized poor and the peasant masses denied the fruits of any agrarian revolution.

Chapters 2 and 3 deal with the *economic* management of the crisis of contemporary world capitalism.

The crisis expresses itself in the fact that the profits derived from production do not find sufficient outlets in the form of lucrative investments capable of further developing productive capacity. Management of the crisis therefore involves finding other outlets for this excess of floating capital, so that its sudden devalorization can be avoided.

At national level, such management compels neoliberal policies that are perfectly rational from this point of view. Of course, they lock the economies into deflationary spirals of stagnation, which is what makes them policies for merely managing or containing, rather than solving, the crisis.

In addition, globalization requires that management of the crisis should also operate at the world level. The Bretton Woods institutions – notably the International Monetary Fund (IMF) and the World Bank – have been made to serve this purpose, so that the economies of the South and the East are subordinated to these imperatives. The restructuring programmes imposed in this context are not at all what their name, structural adjustment, would suggest. The idea behind them is not to change structures in a way that might allow a new general boom and market expansion, but only to make conjunctural adjustments that obey the short-term logic of assuring the financial profitability of the surplus capital. Naturally such world crisis-management proves untenable: it multiplies the number of conflicts that it is unable to regulate, all the more because it operates within the framework of an obsolete monetary system.

Chapter 4 considers various questions relating to *political* management of the chaos produced by the utopian and unrealistic project of 'running the world like a market'.

Until very recent times, the space of economic management of capital accumulation coincided with that of its political and social dimensions. This national bourgeois state provided the model of modernity that the Third World sought to reproduce after the Second World War, through the model of autocentred national development (albeit open to the international economy) and construction/modernization of the state. In this context, the (often multi-ethnic) ruling classes of Asia, Africa and Eastern Europe based their legitimacy upon the economic development that the strong expansion of world capitalism favoured until the 1980s.

Deepening globalization has put an end to this coincidence of spaces. A new contradiction now characterizes world capitalism: on the one hand, the centres of gravity of the economic forces commanding accumulation have shifted outside the frontiers of individual states; on the other hand, there is no political, social, ideological and cultural framework at world level that can give coherence to the overall management of the system. In its political dimension, then, management of the crisis consists in trying to suppress the second term of the contradiction – the state – in such a way as to impose management of society by 'the market' as the only rule. Sweeping anti-state ideologies and practices form part of this logic.

Erosion of the old growth models has therefore plunged the peripheral countries of the South and East into a crisis of the nation-state, reviving centrifugal movements with an often ethnic expression. The crisis has shattered the unity of the ruling classes of the periphery, so that rival fractions now try to base their legitimacy upon the ethnic aspirations of their disoriented people. Management of this crisis – through manipulation of democratic aspirations and national rights – fuels the project of subordinating societies to the demands of the market, which presupposes the destruction of states capable of modulating effectively the conditions of globalization.

Chapters 5, 6 and 7 take up aspects of the quest for an alternative to total submission to the logic of capital.

In record time, the pursuit of the liberal utopia has produced results so catastrophic that its discourse is already losing momentum. The wind is starting to change direction, to blow on the side of reason.

Contrary to all currently prevailing crisis-management policies, it is necessary to rethink development as a societal model. For growth is not the natural product of market management and expansion policies; it is the possible result of transformation policies that have been thought through in all their dimensions.

The postwar expansion was produced by a strategic adjustment of capital to the social conditions that popular democratic forces, flushed with the victory over fascism in 1945, were able to impose upon it. It was the exact opposite of the so-called adjustment policies of our own day. Whatever certain university professors may imagine, history is not infallibly directed by the laws of 'pure economics'. It is produced by social reactions to the tendencies implied by those laws, reactions that in turn define the concrete social relations within which the laws operate. 'Anti-systemic' forces – in other words, the organized, consistent and effective refusal to bow completely to the exigencies of those supposed laws – do just as much as the 'pure' logic of capital accumulation to shape real history. They determine the possibilities and forms of the expansion taking place within the organized framework that they themselves impose.

Our aim here is to provide a systematic critique of the simplistic ruling discourse about the ineluctability of globalization. It must be recognized that interdependence has to be negotiated: that nationally necessary forms of development have to be framed and supported, and that initial inequalities have to be corrected rather than left to grow more profound. To recognize these necessities, then, is to understand that development is not synonymous with market expansion. But the dominant discourse always refuses to make this distinction. It implies that market expansion necessarily 'leads to' social progress and democracy, and that the 'difficulties' (the 'pockets' of poverty, unemployment and social marginalization, as they are called) are really only 'transitory'. No one gives much thought to whether the transition will last a few years or several centuries!

Keeping these points in mind, Chapter 5 deals with aspects of any future revival of Third World development, Chapter 6 with the challenges facing the construction of Europe, and Chapter 7 with the responsibilities of Third World intellectuals.

CHAPTER 1

The Future of Global Polarization

Unequal Development and the Historical Forms of Capitalism

History since antiquity has been characterized by the unequal development of regions. But it is only in the modern era that polarization has become the immanent byproduct of the integration of the entire planet into the capitalist system.

Modern (capitalist) polarization has appeared in successive forms during the evolution of the capitalist mode of production:

(1) **The mercantilist form** (1500–1800) before the industrial revolution which was fashioned by the hegemony of merchant capital in the dominant Atlantic centres, and by the creation of the peripheral zones (the Americas) whose function involved their total compliance with the logic of accumulation of merchant capital.

(2) **The so-called classical model** which grew out of the industrial revolution and henceforth defined the basic forms of capitalism. In contrast, the peripheries – progressively all of Asia (except for Japan) and Africa, which were added to Latin America – remained rural, non-industrialized, and as a result their participation in the world division of labour took place via agriculture and mineral production. This important characteristic of polarization was accompanied by a second equally important one: the crystallization of core industrial systems as national autocentred systems which paralleled the construction of the national bourgeois states. Taken together, these two characteristics account for the dominant lines of the ideology of national liberation which was the response to the challenge of polarization: (i) the goal of industrialization as a synonym for a liberating progress and as a means of 'catching up'; (ii) the goal

of constructing nation-states inspired by the models of those in the core. This is how modernization ideology was conceived. From the industrial revolution (after 1800) up to the end of the Second World War the world system was characterized by this classical form of polarization.

(3) **The postwar period** (1945–90) witnessed the progressive erosion of the above two characteristics. It was a period of industrialization of the peripheries, unequal and uneven to be sure. It was the dominant factor in Asia and Latin America, with the national liberation movement doing its best to accelerate the process within peripheral states which had recently regained their political autonomy. This period was simultaneously, however, one of the progressive dismantling of autocentric national production systems and their recomposition as constitutive elements of an integrated world production system. This double erosion was the new manifestation of the deepening of globalization.

(4) **The most recent period** (since 1990) in which the accumulation of these transformations has resulted in the collapse of the equilibria characteristic of the postwar world system.

This evolution is not leading simply to a new world order characterized by new forms of polarization, but to global disorder. The chaos which confronts us today comes from, a triple failure of the system: (i) it has not developed new forms of political and social organization going beyond the nation-state – a new requirement of the globalized system of production; (ii) it has not developed economic and political relationships capable of reconciling the rise of industrialization in the newly competitive peripheral zones of Asia and Latin America with the pursuit of global growth; (iii) it has not developed a relationship, other than an exclusionary one, with the African periphery which is not engaged in competitive industrialization at all. This chaos is visible in all regions of the world and in all facets of the political, social and ideological crisis. It is at the root of the difficulties in the present construction of Europe and that continent's inability to pursue market integration and establish parallel integrative political structures. It is also the cause of the convulsions in all the peripheries in Eastern Europe, in the old semi-industrialized Third World and in the new marginalized Fourth World. Far from sustaining the progression of globalization, the current chaos reveals its extreme vulnerability.

The predominance of this chaos should not keep us from thinking about alternative scenarios for a new 'world order' even if there are many different possible future 'world orders'. What I am trying to do here is to call attention to questions which have been glossed over by the triumphalism of inevitable globalization at the same time as its precariousness is revealed.

The reader will no doubt have discovered that this analysis of world capitalism is not centred on the question of hegemonies. I do not subscribe to the successive hegemonies school of historiography. The concept of hegemony is often sterile, and is unscientific because it has been so loosely defined. It does not seem to me that it should be the centre of the debate. I have, in contrast, developed the idea that hegemony is the exception to the rule. The rule is conflict among partners which puts an end to hegemony. The hegemony of the United States, seemingly unchallenged today, perhaps by default, is as fragile and precarious as the globalization of the structures through which it operates.

The Present World System and the Five Monopolies of the Centre

In my opinion, the debate should start with an in-depth discussion of the new features in the present world system which are produced by the erosion of the previous one. In my opinion there are two new elements:

(1) The erosion of the autocentred nation-state and the subsequent disappearance of the link between the arena of reproduction and accumulation together with the weakening of political and social control which up to now had been defined precisely by the frontiers of this autocentred nation-state;

(2) The erosion of the great divide: industrialized centre/non-industrialized peripheral regions, and the emergence of new dimensions of polarization.

A country's position in the global hierarchy is defined by its capacity to compete in the world market. Recognizing this truism does not in any way imply sharing the bourgeois economist's view that this position is achieved as the result of rational measures – the said rationality being assessed by the yardstick of the so-called 'objective laws of the market'. On the contrary, I think that this competitiveness is a complex product of many economic, political and social factors. In this unequal fight the centres use what I call their 'five monopolies'. These monopolies constitute a challenge to social theory in its totality. They are:

(1) **Technological monopoly**. This requires huge expenditures that only a large and wealthy state can envisage. Without the support of the state, especially through military spending – something liberal discourse doesn't mention – most of these monopolies would not last.

(2) **Financial control of worldwide financial markets**. These monopolies have an unprecedented efficacy thanks to the liberalization of the rules governing their establishment. Not so long ago, the greater part of a nation's savings could circulate only within the largely national arena of its financial institutions. Today these savings are handled centrally by the institutions whose operations are worldwide. We are talking of finance capital: capital's most globalized component. Despite this, the logic of this globalization of finance could be called into question by a simple political decision to delink, even if delinking were limited to the domain of financial transfers. Moreover I think that the rules governing the free movement of finance capital have broken down. This system had been based in the past on the free floating of currencies on the market (according to the theory that money is a commodity like any other) with the dollar serving *de facto* as a universal currency. Regarding money as a commodity, however, is a theory that is unscientific and the pre-eminent position of the dollar is only *faute de mieux*. A national currency cannot fulfil the functions of an international currency unless there is a surplus of exports in the country whose currency purports to serve as an international currency, thus underwriting structural adjustment in the other countries. This was the case with Great Britain in the late-nineteenth century. This is not the case of the United States today which actually finances its deficit by the borrowing which the rest of the world is forced to accept. Nor indeed is this the case with the competitors of the United States: Japan's surplus (that of Germany disappeared after reunification in 1991) is not sufficient to meet the financial needs occasioned by the structural adjustment of the others. Under these conditions financial globalization, far from being a 'natural' process, is an extremely fragile one. In the short run, it leads only to permanent instability rather than to the stability necessary for the efficient operation of the processes of adjustment.

(3) **Monopolistic access to the planet's natural resources**. The dangers of the reckless exploitation of these resources are now planet-wide. Capitalism, based on short-term rationality, cannot overcome these dangers posed by this reckless behaviour, and it therefore reinforces the monopolies of already developed countries. The much-vaunted environmental concern of these countries is simply not to let others be equally irresponsible.

(4) **Media and communication monopolies**. These not only lead to uniformity of culture but also open up new means of political manipulation. The expansion of the modern media market is already one of the major components in the erosion of democratic practices in the West itself.

(5) **Monopolies over weapons of mass destruction**. Held in check by the postwar bipolarity, this monopoly is again, as in 1945, the sole domain of the United States. While it may be true that nuclear proliferation risks getting out of control, it is still the only way of fighting this unacceptable US monopoly in the absence of democratic international control.

These five monopolies, taken as a whole, define the framework within which the law of globalized value operates. The law of value is the condensed expression of all these conditions, and not the expression of objective, 'pure' economic rationality. The conditioning of all of these processes annuls the impact of industrialization in the peripheries, devalues their productive work and overestimates the supposed value-added resulting from the activities of the new monopolies from which the centres profit. What results is a new hierarchy, more unequal than ever before, in the distribution of income on a world scale, subordinating the industries of the peripheries and reducing them to the role of subcontracting. This is the new foundation of polarization, presaging its future forms.

An Alternative Humanist Project of Globalization

In contrast to the dominant ideological discourse, I maintain that globalization via the market, is a reactionary utopia. We must counter it by developing an alternative humanistic project of globalization consistent with a socialist perspective.

Implied in the realization of such a project is the construction of a global political system which is not in the service of a global market, but one which defines its parameters in the same way as the nation-state represented historically the social framework of the national market and not merely its passive field of deployment. A global political system would thus have major responsibilities in each of the following four areas:

(1) The organization of global disarmament at appropriate levels, thus liberating humanity from the menace of nuclear and other holocausts.

(2) The organization of access to the planet's resources in an equitable manner so that there would be less inequality. There would have to be a global decision-making process with a valuation (tariffication) of resources which would make obligatory waste reduction and the more equitable distribution of the value and income from these resources. This could also be the beginning of a globalized fiscal system.

(3) Negotiation of open, flexible economic relationships between the world's major regions which, currently, are unequally developed. This would reduce progressively the centres' technological and financial monopolies. This means, of course, the liquidation of the institutions presently running the global market (the so-called World Bank, the IMF, the World Trade Organization etc.) and the creation of other systems for managing the global economy.

(4) Starting negotiation for the correct management of the global/national dialectic in the areas of communication, culture and political policy. This implies the creation of political institutions which would represent social interests on a global scale – the beginning of a 'world parliament' going beyond the inter-state mechanisms of the United Nations system that exist now.

Obstacles to the Realization of this Project

It is more than evident that current trends are not going in the direction described above and that humanist objectives are not those being fought for today. I am not surprised. The erosion of the old system of globalization is not able to prepare its own succession and can only lead to chaos. Dominant forces are developing their activities in the framework of these constraints, trying to manoeuvre for short-term gain and thereby aggravating the chaos. Their attempt to legitimate their choices by the stale ideology of the 'self-regulating' market, or by affirming that 'there is no alternative', or by pure and simple cynicism, is not the solution but part of the problem. The people's spontaneous responses to the degradation they experience, however, are not necessarily any more helpful. In a time of disarray, illusory solutions such as fundamentalism or chauvinism can be highly politically mobilizing. It is up to the Left – that is in fact its historic mission – to formulate, in theory and in practice, a humanistic response to the challenge. In its absence and until it is formulated, regressive and outright criminal scenarios will be the most likely order of the day.

The difficulties confronting the EU's European project right now are a good illustration of the impasse created by globalization through market mechanisms. In the first flush of enthusiasm over the European project no one foresaw these difficulties. Yet they were perfectly predictable by people who never believed that the Common Market by itself could create a united Europe. They said that a project as ambitious as this could not be accomplished without a Left capable of making it socially and culturally progressive. In the absence of that, it would remain fragile, and even a minor political accident could prove fatal. It was necessary, therefore, for the various European Lefts to make sure that each step of the integration was accompanied by a double series of measures: on the one hand, ensuring that profits went to the workers, thereby reinforcing their social power and their unity; and on the other, beginning the construction of a political system which would supersede the nation-state and could be the only unit that could effectively manage an enlarged market. This did not happen. The European project, in the hands of the Right, was reduced to purely mercantilist proportions, and the Left sooner or later simply offered its support without imposing any conditions. The result is what we see before us: the economic downturn has put the European partners in an adversarial position. They can only imagine solutions to their problems (notably unemployment) that are at the expense of others, and they don't even have effective tools for achieving those. They are increasingly tempted to retreat behind national barriers. Even the sincere efforts to avoid such action on the part of French and German politicians on both the Right and the Left have resulted only in rhetoric rather than effective pan-European action.

The EU's Europe is experiencing problems at the same time as the wider Europe is giving a new meaning to the challenge facing it. This ought to be an opportunity for the Left to rethink the European project as a whole and to begin the construction of a confederal political and economic 'big' Europe that is anchored on the left by a reconstructed and united European labour force. But it has missed this opportunity and, on the contrary, has backed the forces of the Right which were in a hurry to profit from the collapse of the Soviet Empire by substituting a kind of unrestrained, wildcat capitalism. It is obvious that the present Latin Americanization of Eastern Europe can only weaken the chances of success of a left-leaning pan-European project. That in turn can only accentuate the disequilibrium within the Europe of the EU to the benefit of the only partner able to profit from this evolution: a reunited Germany.

The crisis of the European project is one of the major challenges confronting the construction of the new globalization. But these inward-looking manifestations, these inadequate and tragic responses to the challenge of the construction of a renewed global system, are not found exclusively in Europe. They are seen throughout the former Third World, especially in regions marginalized by the collapse of the old world order (sub-Saharan Africa and the Arab Islamic areas), and also in the new Third World of the East (as in the former USSR and former Yugoslavia), where we see self-destructive involutions rather than valid responses to the challenge.

Possible Future Scenarios and their Inadequacy

Given this background, there are a few realistic scenarios which can be proposed. I will examine several of them and show that they do not constitute adequate responses to the demands posed by the construction of an acceptable and stable world order. They therefore do not provide a way out from chaos.

The European question is at the centre of theorizing about the future of globalization. With the breakdown of the European project and the threat of its disintegration, forces faithful to the European idea could find it useful, and possible, to regroup around their second best position, that is, a German Europe. There is reason to believe that in this scenario the British ship would sail close to American shores, keeping its distance from 'continental Europe'. We have already started down this path and some have even legitimated this choice by giving priority to the notion of the 'neutral management of money' (a technocratic concept based on ignorance of the political meaning of monetary management), and conferring it (where else?) on the Bundesbank! I do not believe that this caricature of the original European project can be truly stable since several European countries will not accept the erosion of their positions which it implies.

To make matters worse, the preferential position of the United States is not challenged by this scenario of a German-led Europe. Nor is it clear that there is anything in this project that could challenge America in any of the areas of the five monopolies discussed above. A German-led Europe would remain within the American orbit.

There is another possible scenario – for lack of an alternative – a kind of second edition, American hegemony. There are many variations of this. The most likely one is a 'sharing of the burden' associated with neo-imperialist regionalization: hitching Latin America to the US wagon and Africa to the German–European one (with some crumbs for France), and with the Gulf oil region and a 'common market of the Middle East' remaining the domain of the United States. The American presence is already felt by its military occupation of the Gulf and less directly by its alliance with Israel. Finally, there might be a certain symmetry, with South and South-East Asia left open to Japanese expansion. But there is no equality implied in this division among the three centres: the United States would retain its privileged position. Here, too, I do not believe that neo-imperialist options of this kind would guarantee the stability of the system. They would be disputed periodically by revolts in Latin America, Asia and Africa.

We should therefore focus our attention on Asia, which has been largely outside the Euro-American conflict. It has often been observed that Asia – from Japan to Communist China, Korea, and to a lesser degree certain countries of South-East Asia (Singapore, Thailand and Malaysia) and even India – has not been affected by the present crisis, and that these countries have registered successes in terms of growth and efficiency (measured by their competitive position on the world market). Nevertheless, one cannot leap ahead and say that Asia will be the locus of the next hegemony. Asia may have more than half the world's population, but this is divided among distinct states. In place of a vague concept of global hegemony, one could substitute the notion of Asia becoming the principal region of capitalist accumulation. It remains to be described in detail how this may be occurring already: the articulation between the different Asian nations, and between them and the rest of the world. And there are variants of this model. The easiest to imagine – the domination of the region by Japanese imperialism – is, in my opinion, the least plausible. Admirers of Japan's recent success too often underestimate Japan's vulnerability. It is because of this weakness that Japan remains tied to the US. Nor is it probable that China, or even Korea, would accept being subordinated to Japan. Under these conditions the maintenance of an inter-Asian equilibrium would depend on forces external to the region, and here again only the United States is a candidate for this role, which would in turn prolong its primacy on the world scene.

Nonetheless it is highly probable that the positions of these Asian countries will be reinforced within the capitalist world system. How will the United States react to this? All alliance strategies will, in my opinion, revolve around this question. It goes almost without saying that the future development of China threatens all global equilibria. And that is why the United States will feel threatened by her development. In my opinion the United States and China will be *the* major antagonists in any future global conflict.

Renewing a Perspective of Global Socialism

Current developments suggest different possible scenarios, none of which questions the realities of North–South polarization. The commanding logic of the capitalist system perpetuates the centre/periphery polarization. Its modes of operation are ever renewed and will in the future be founded on the five monopolies around which I have constructed my argument.

One could say that there is nothing new in this view because polarization is almost part of the natural order of things. I do not agree with this contention precisely because this polarization has been challenged over the past five centuries. Peoples peripheralized by capitalist world expansion, and who seemed for a long time to accept their fate, have over the past 50 years ceased accepting it, and they will refuse to do so more and more in the future. The positive political aspect of the universalization which capitalism inaugurated – and which can't get beyond its present truncated version – is the worm in the fruit. The Russian and Chinese revolutions began the attempt to go beyond the system on the basis of the revolts of peripheral people, and this will be continued in new versions. The final explanation for the instability of the world-system being built is found here. Of course, the conflicts that will occupy international attention in the future will, as always, not all be of equal importance. I would intuitively give determining priority to those involving the peoples of Asia and the dominant system. This doesn't mean others won't participate in this generalized revolt against polarization, just as it does not mean that transformations, and even progress, won't emanate from the very centres of the system.

In short, a humanistic response to the challenge of globalization inaugurated by capitalist expansion may be idealistic but it is not utopian. On the contrary, it is the only realistic project possible. If only we begin to develop it, powerful social forces will rally to it from all regions of the world.

This is the way to renew the perspective of global socialism. In preparation, ideological and political forces must regroup in order to be capable of combating the five monopolies which reproduce capitalism. This struggle will create conditions for mutual adjustment. In it we have to reconsider fundamental questions on the ideological cultural front: (i) the dialectic between the universal and the particular; (ii) the relationship between political democracy and social progress; (iii) the dialectic of so-called economic efficiency (and the way it is expressed, 'the market') and values of equality and fraternity; and (iv) the definition of a global socialist objective in the light of all the above.

On the political front we have to develop world organizational forms which are more authentically democratic so as to be capable of reshaping economic relations on the basis of diminishing inequality. In this perspective it seems to me that high priority should be given to reorganizing the global system around large areas which would group together scattered parts of the peripheries. This would be the place for the constitution of Latin American, Arab, African, South-East Asian regions, alongside China and India (the only continental countries on our planet). I propose that this objective receive priority treatment in any new agenda of the Non-Aligned Movement. These regional groupings do not exclude others, such as Europe or the former USSR. The reason for this political call is simple: it is only by operating on this scale that one can effectively combat the five monopolies of our analysis. The construction, in turn, of a truly global economic and financial system becomes possible on this basis.

Of course the transformation of the world always begins by struggles at its base. Without changes in ideological, political and social systems at the national level, any discussion about challenging globalization and polarization remains a dead letter.

This chapter contains in condensed form conclusions from discussions developed in:

Empire of Chaos (Monthly Review, 1983)
Re-reading the Post War Period (Monthly Review, 1994)
L'ethnicité à l'assaut des nations (L'Harmattan, 1993)
Mondialisation et accumulation (L'Harmattan, 1993)

CHAPTER 2

The Capitalist Economic Management of the Crisis of Contemporary Society

The action of major world economic institutions, especially the IMF, the World Bank group and GATT-WTO, has been the object of many critical studies. So many of these studies are outstanding both in the precision of their information and the accuracy of their analysis that one may wonder if anything more needs to be said. It is noticeable, however, that until around 1980 most of these criticisms remained evenhanded. Of course, critics pointed out that the policies pursued by these institutions were part of the logic of capitalist expansion, serving the interests of transnationals, careless of the environment (whose claims had barely begun to be gauged), uncritically accepting the idea that 'development' would bring about a decrease in 'pockets of poverty' by a 'trickle-down' effect. Yet, on the other hand, a positive view was taken of openness and the progress of globalization, and consequently of the support countries received from the IMF to help solve balance-of-payments difficulties, return to the convertibility of major currencies and gradually lower tariffs. It was noted also that these institutions respected the national options of states choosing to assign a major economic role to the public sector, to subject foreign capital to strict controls and, even, in some cases, to opt for 'socialism' and delink their internal prices and wages from the logic of world capitalism, systematically redistributing national income.

At the time, therefore, one of the main criticisms addressed to these institutions was the timidity of their interventions. It was seen as regrettable, for example, that the IMF should be helpless in its relations with the great capitalist powers, that the United States should have eliminated the World Bank from European reconstruction and used the alternative of the Marshall Plan, that GATT-WTO should plead for lower tariffs without daring to go any further.

The external debt crisis, which opened with Mexico's threat to suspend payments in 1982, did not radically change this perspective. The institutions – and especially the IMF, one of the main parties involved – were criticized above all for their inaction in relation to the new situation: the Fund merely organized the 'rescheduling' of the debt, without tackling its causes or the mechanisms ensuring its reproduction and expansion (high interest rates, uncontrolled openness, etc.).

Criticisms addressed to international economic institutions became much more severe in 1981. At that point, when Ronald Reagan – for whom extreme neoliberal doctrines were gospel – came to power, the institutions became instant converts to these doctrines, as if it was necessary for them to follow every change of fashion inside the White House. This conversion immediately crystallized as a simple and universal programme for action known as the 'structural adjustment programme', or SAP. The programme was first applied to Third World countries considered to be in crisis (as if the capitalist countries were not!); it compelled them to 'adjust' – unilaterally – to new conditions. At the end of the 1980s the SAP was extended to Eastern-bloc countries to 'help' them through a swift reconversion to 'normal' capitalism.

I shall not enumerate here the many criticisms that have been made of this 'adjustment' programme in its various forms. Excellent and comprehensive critiques, including both concrete studies of national experiences and broad syntheses, have been carried out in such a way that there is no need to repeat them. I have no hesitation in going along with the summary of these criticisms formulated by the International People's Tribunal to Judge the G7 in their Tokyo verdict of 1993. According to the tribunal, the general consequences of SAPs have been: a sharp increase in unemployment, a fall in the remuneration of work, an increase in food dependency, a grave deterioration of the environment, a deterioration in healthcare systems, a fall in admissions to educational institutions, a decline in the productive capacity of many nations, the sabotage of democratic systems, and the continued growth of external debt.

This judgement – graphic, yet accurate and healthy – contains two forceful and important conclusions, the first explicit and the second implicit: (i) the policies instituted by international institutions in obedience to strategies adopted by the G7 are the cause of the brutal and massive impoverishment of popular majorities, particularly in the South and East; and (ii) these policies do not provide any solution to the general crisis of contemporary society; on the contrary, they aggravate its development by feeding into a deflationist spiral.

This second aspect of the judgement strikes me as most important for the argument I will be presenting below. For the most part, criticisms have been formulated by what are known as NGOs of an extremely diverse nature. The concept of capitalism is unknown to many of them, and as a consequence their criticisms are strictly moral. The policies are accused of fostering poverty, as if the logic of the system had nothing to do with it. Poverty is thus seen as the product of 'errors' which could be 'corrected'.

Some critics, it is true, do not ignore the responsibilities belonging to the logic of the system as a whole and, indeed, over the past few years, the World Bank has attempted to restore its reputation by offering a limited self-criticism of the neoliberal policies favoured during the 1980s. A malicious mind would be tempted to say that the World Bank is simply adapting to the new rhetoric of the Clinton White House. However that may be, neither the IMF, hidden behind monetary professionalism, nor GATT-WTO, ever opaque and shielded by the 'commercial secrets' of the transnationals which dominate its clientele, have followed suit. Again, malicious tongues might be tempted to comment that this double language is also that of the White House and that officials from the various institutions have simply distributed the work in this spirit.

In any case, the Bank's self-criticism, and the tears it sheds over the plight of the poor, do not deceive all of its readers. In a 1993 document, Marcos Arruda, general secretary of the International Committee for Voluntary Agencies (ICVA), ironically made the following points: the World Bank continues to ignore the fact that the poor were not on the agenda of the policies carried out before 1980, and were not, therefore, a 'new' issue; the debt crisis has yet to be resolved, with the South, as a consequence, having become an exporter of capital to the North; that the export-oriented growth advocated by the Bank is fragile and unsustainable; and that it is the nature of SAPs to exclude popular participation and democracy.

The 'Laws of History': Capitalist Expansion Not Synonymous with Development

I believe that it is always useful to recapitulate the logic of capitalism, even at the risk of repeating truisms. Capitalism is not 'a system of development' that might be opposed, for instance, to the 'socialist doctrine'. I think it is necessary to make a distinction here between the reality of what capitalism produces, i.e., the expansion of capital, and the concept of development. The first phenomenon, studied as a social reality, must be considered on two levels, that of its immanent (abstract) tendency and that of its historical (concrete) reality. The concept of development, on the other hand, is by nature ideological. It enables one to judge results according to criteria that have been drawn up *a priori* – the same criteria that contribute to the definition of a social project. Such projects may be more or less radical, put forth different concepts of freedom or equality, human liberation, efficiency, etc.

The combination (or the confusion) of these two concepts – the reality (capitalist expansion) and what is desirable (development in a predefined direction) – is the cause of many blind spots in the criticisms of existing policies. The institutions with which we are dealing amalgamate the concept systematically – they propose ways of helping capital to expand, and identify the result, or what could be the result according to them, as development.

Yet the logic of capitalist expansion does not imply any result that can be identified in terms of development. For example, it does not imply full employment, or a predetermined degree of equality in the distribution of income. Expansion is guided by the search for profit by companies (or more precisely by the bourgeoisie that controls them and is endowed, for this purpose, with the monopoly represented by private property). This logic may cause employment to expand under some conditions, or to contract under others; it may reduce income inequalities or accentuate them.

Again, the confusion entertained between the concepts of 'market economy' and 'capitalist economy' is the cause of a dangerous weakening of the criticisms aimed at existing policies. 'The market', a term referring by nature to competition, is not 'capitalism', of which the content is defined precisely by the limits to competition implied by the monopoly of private property (belonging to some while others are excluded). 'The market' and capitalism are two distinct concepts. Walras, who was consistent in his defence of the 'advantages' of the market, did not entertain the confusion which our students of neoliberalism unconsciously perpetrate every day. Even Walras grasped the fact that capitalism offers a non-optimal version of the market, and that the true rule of the market implies the abolition of private property. Therefore, he imagined an ideal of 'capitalism without capitalists' – a concept formulated by Engels to describe the project of the Second International, and taken up by the post-Stalinist Soviet 'reformers' of the Novossibirsk school. The utopian nature of this project, whose deficiencies were confirmed by the failure of the subsequent Soviet reform known as market socialism, merely reminds us of the criticism addressed by Marx to economism.

The fact is that actually existing capitalism does not work as a system of competition between the beneficiaries of the monopoly of property among themselves and against others. In order to work, capitalism requires the intervention of a collective authority representing capital as a whole. Therefore, the state cannot be separated from capitalism. The policies of capital, and hence of the state acting as representative of capital, have their own (concrete) logic of stages. These forms of logic explain why the expansion of capital causes employment to expand at certain moments and to contract at others. Such forms of logic are not the expression of abstract 'market laws', but requirements of the profitability of capital under certain historical conditions. The rise of unemployment over the past twenty-five years has been produced not by the market, but by the strategies of capital.

Unemployment is desired by the capitalist state as a necessary means to destroy the achievements of the workers' movement. This proposition applies both to the developed capitalist West and to the reconquered countries of the East. There is no reason to believe the speeches of those in power as they lament unemployment. In the peripheries of the capitalist system, poverty and unequal distribution of income are not negative effects produced by specific circumstances or mistaken policies. They are the product of the system's logic, the logic of world polarization immanent in the system itself. Therefore these effects are permanent, even though they are diminished in certain phases and increased in others.

During the period with which we are concerned (the post-Second World War period from 1945 to 1994), the logic of capitalist expansion, on the one hand, gradually eroded national systems of production created by the previous historical period (since mercantilism and especially the industrial revolution), and, on the other hand, adapted to the progressive industrialization of the peripheries, which until then had precisely been excluded from the field of industrial production.

Capitalist expansion both produced these changes in the world system and adjusted itself to them. I suggest, therefore, that the policies carried out first by states and second by international institutions should be examined in the light of this twofold requirement that is both complementary and contradictory. The consequence I see is that moral judgements, or those expressed in closely related terms such as success and failure, should be revised from the point of view of this logic instead of being based on results achieved in terms of development.

My conception of the 'laws of history', as expressed here by the logic of capitalist expansion, is not determinist. For example, the industrialization of the periphery during the postwar period is not the natural product of capitalist expansion, but the product of conditions created by the victories of national liberation imposed by industrialization, and to which worldwide capital adapted. Another example: the erosion of the effectiveness of the national state produced by capitalist globalization is not a decisive and irreversible determinant of the future. On the contrary, national reactions to this globalization may compel world expansion to take unforeseen directions.

The reflections developed here require a detailed examination of the postwar period, identification of its successive phases, and within this context an assessment of the policies carried out by the institutions under consideration, either to support capitalist expansion or to help it adapt to the conditions imposed on it by the social relations specific to the period, which as a whole is divided into a period of prosperity (1945–75) and a period of crisis starting in 1975. According to my analysis, the prosperity of the first was founded on the complementarity of three social projects: (i) the national social-democratic project of the welfare state, basing its action on the efficiency of interdependent national systems; (ii) what I have designated as the 'Bandung Project' after the conference held in 1955 at which the Non-Aligned Movement and the goal of Third World modernization and industrialization first took shape, involving national bourgeois construction at the periphery of the system as the ideology of 'development'; (iii) the Soviet project of capitalism without capitalists, relatively independent of the dominant world system.

During this first period, international institutions carried out obvious functions related to the boom. They helped globalization progress, while avoiding for reasons of principle any challenge to the independence of the components of the system. Their interventions, almost by nature, always brought about a shift to the Right. The second period involved first erosion, then crisis and collapse of the systems that had been the basis of the previous prosperity. This period, which is not yet over, is not a period in which a new world order is being established, as has been asserted too often and too glibly. Instead, it is a period of chaos which is far from being over. This is the context in which I locate the actions of the international institutions after 1970. According to my analysis, these actions are not part of a positive strategy for the expansion of capital; rather they are attempts to create the conditions for this expansion. They will not succeed because the 'spontaneous' project of capitalist domination – the project of managing the world through what is known as the market, that is, the immediate and short-term interests of the dominant forces of capital – remains utopian. This very specific situation invites us to reconsider the spontaneous tendencies of management by capital. From this perspective I believe it is useful to focus on what I have called the five monopolies through which the domination of the centres over the peripheries might develop in the near future (cf. p.4).

The Institutional Structure: The Bretton Woods Institutions

A great deal has been written about the interventions of the large international economic institutions (IMF, World Bank, GATT-WTO, UN institutions), to which should also be added the major regional institutions (including the EC, and for Africa the Lomé Convention governing the association of the European Union with the Caribbean and the Pacific (EC-ACP)). In what follows, I shall recapitulate this history only to emphasize the criticisms most often levelled at these institutions and the inferences I draw from them.

The IMF

The IMF's original mandate was to ensure monetary stability in an open world economy, as a substitute for the gold standard, which had fulfilled this function successfully until the First World War. This implied that the IMF's interventions were to impose adjustments on all parties, whether their payment balances were in surplus or deficit. During the first period of its existence, the IMF gave the impression of a certain efficiency as it helped to re-establish the convertibility of European currencies (1948–57), then helped European economies to adjust (1958–66). From 1967 on, however, the Fund failed to maintain stability despite the creation of SDRs. The adoption of the general system of floating currencies in 1973 may be considered to mark the end of the Bretton Woods mandate. At that point the continued existence of the IMF was called into question. The institution survived by taking on new functions: management of unilateral structural adjustments in developing countries and, from the end of the 1980s, interventions in Eastern-bloc countries to ensure their reincorporation into the international monetary system.

Criticisms addressed to the institution, widely shared by almost all analysts of the world economy, agree on the following points:

(1) The IMF (like the other Bretton Woods institution, the World Bank) was designed to provide the United States with complete control over its interventions. Rejecting the option of a world central bank defended by Keynes, the United States preferred a weaker institution, in a state of dependence, over one that would have been more effective but for which the United States would have had to share responsibility with others. This is why the resources of the IMF have always been limited, despite its borrowing. The IMF may be able to act as a catalyst (by defining the rules of conditionality, for instance), but it cannot go much further.

(2) Despite the logic spelled out in its mandate, the IMF has never been able to compel the great capitalist powers (particularly the United States), whether they show a surplus or a deficit, to carry out structural adjustments as harsh as the ones it imposes on Third World countries. The reason for this, of course, is the one spelled out in the preceding paragraph.

(3) In its relations with the Third World, the IMF did not pursue the objective of either preventing debt from reaching excessive levels during the 1970s or subsequently of reducing this debt. Its job is to manage the debt by imposing structural adjustments designed for

this exclusive purpose (servicing the debt) even if they are detrimental to economic growth.

(4) In its new relations with the countries of the Eastern bloc, the IMF pursues the objective of accelerating their return to convertible currencies in a context of maximum openness. The extreme brutality of the solutions recommended by the Fund has been obvious: convertibility is to be re-established within one year, whereas Western Europe took fifteen years to reach this point after 1945.

(5) In all of these functions, the IMF has no real authority to define objectives. The Fund is merely the executive of strategies defined by the G7 – strategies that are based on the least common denominator among the positions of the United States, Japan and the EC.

It is necessary to go beyond these criticisms if we want a serious discussion of the value of alternative proposals. We must ask if it is possible to correct the weaknesses set out above, and thus to opt for the transformation of the IMF into a genuine world central bank – one that would promote adjustment, of course, but adjustment for all, as part of a strategy for growth and development that would encompass significant effects (growth of employment, decrease in poverty and so on), as well as respect for the environment, a reduction of inequalities at the global level and openness. I doubt it, for the following reasons:

(1) The successive phases of growth and stagnation characteristic of the history of capitalism are not produced by a monetary system that is 'good' in one case and 'bad' in the other. I have argued (along with Baran and Sweezy) that capitalism tends, by nature, to create relative overproduction and that the tendency to stagnation associated with this overproduction is overcome, during the growth phases, for reasons specific to each period. For the postwar period, these circumstances are the ones I have analysed as a three-part system, consisting of: national 'Fordism'; European reconstruction and developmentalism; national liberation, Sovietism, and 'delinking', all reinforced by the gigantic military spending of the period. The strong overall growth produced by these conditions made the monetary system work more smoothly, whatever its vagaries.

(2) Under these conditions, exchange rate stability was produced not by the adequacy of the Bretton Woods system but, at first, by the economic power of the United States. This power, manifesting itself as 'hunger for dollars', was reinforced by the dollar's gold convertibility and by administrative controls on capital movements in Europe, which were maintained until reconstruction was completed and Europe was in a position to become open. This movement continued, to the detriment of the United States (hence its relative decline), and the world system went from a shortage to an excess availability of dollars. At the same time, a crisis began with the erosion of the basis of postwar prosperity in the late 1960s (before the first oil shock of 1973), leading to the collapse of opportunities for productive investment. The concomitance of the US deficit (leading to an excess of dollars available on the market) and the crisis of productive investment produced a mass of floating capital with no place to go. The choice of floating exchange rates in 1973 was therefore perfectly rational: it allowed this gigantic mass of floating capital to find an outlet in financial speculation. Today, while world trade is valued at US$2 billion, international capital movements are estimated at US$50 billion! Without financial openness and floating exchange rates, the dead weight represented by this mass would have aggravated the crisis. The logic of the system therefore requires today's focus on 'managing' the crisis rather than on ending it, which the system is not capable of by itself.

(3) Adjustment policies unilaterally imposed on the weakest partners (the Third World and the Eastern block) fulfil this requirement for management of the crisis. They are not mistakes or aberrations produced by following an absurd ideology. The IMF did nothing to prevent the excessive borrowing of the 1970s because the rising debt was very useful as a means of managing the crisis and the overabundance of idle capital which it produced. The logic of adjustment now being carried out requires, therefore, that the free mobility of capital prevail, even if this should cause demand to contract because of reductions in wages and social spending, the liberalization of prices and elimination of subsidies, devaluation, etc., and thus bring about a regression in the possibilities for development. The ritual statements made by these institutions which, in practice, place management of the crisis over every other consideration, the tears that they shed over the plight of the 'poor', their incantations in favour of 'stimulating supply', are nothing but rhetoric, and there is no reason to believe them sincere or find them

credible.

(4) High interest rates are not a mistake. They are the most effective way to ensure an acceptable return for floating capital, given the insurance such capital requires against the exchange risks involved in the flexible system that has been set up. All this constitutes a coherent set of policies for managing the crisis.

(5) Therefore, I do not consider that blame attaches to the IMF. The Bretton Woods institutions were adapted to and supported the postwar boom based on the complementary three-part system mentioned above. When this system entered a crisis, the Bretton Woods system collapsed. The option chosen to deal with the new situation (floating currencies, high interest rates and liberalization of capital flows) has provided, up to now, for effective management of the crisis (from the viewpoint of capital). At the same time, it enables the United States to give its hegemony a new lease on life, by maintaining the international role of the dollar, for lack of an alternative, and by allowing the United States to cover its deficit by forced borrowings from its partners. This option is far from being irrational; it espouses perfectly US interests by providing for the (costly) maintenance of the country's hegemonic military position. There is a striking analogy between what is happening today and what happened when Great Britain lost its dominant economic position. England ceased to be the most efficient industrial power around 1880, but the sterling standard survived throughout the country's long decline until 1931. This allows us to understand the striking and accurate analogy drawn by Walter Russell Mead between the operation of the present system, in which servicing the debt is placed above every other consideration, and the attitude of the victors at Versailles after the First World War. I believe that the analogy extends even further, and that it concerns more than attitudes towards international debt.

(6) Interventions in the countries of the East are dictated by political logic. The brutality of the measures adopted is aimed at clear political objectives: to dismantle the productive structures of the countries of Eastern Europe and the former USSR in order to reincorporate them into world capitalism as subordinate peripheries, and not as equal partners; to demoralize the working classes; and to reinforce the new comprador bourgeoisie. The aim is also to dismantle these countries themselves – the USSR, Yugoslavia, Czechoslovakia – and

to break the ties of economic solidarity among them. This is why, while the Marshall Plan supported the first steps toward the construction of what was to become the EEC and encouraged cooperation among the countries in Eastern Europe, Western policy has aimed to accelerate the disintegration of the former CEMA (better known as Comecon, the nickname popularized by the CIA), even if this should make the reconversion of the regional economies more difficult.

On the basis of these considerations, I do not think that the central proposal of the reformers, namely the transformation of the IMF into a world central bank, is realistic. The idea is certainly logical. Globalization has eroded the power of national states, and therefore demands a globalized management of economic, financial and monetary systems. But the inference drawn from recognition of the fact of globalization, when stated in this way, is inadequate. No economy exists without politics and without a state. Therefore, economic globalization logically requires the construction of a world political system able to respond to the challenge, a power system capable of managing social compromises at the worldwide level, just as national states manage them at their level. However, sufficient maturity does not exist in the area, not even among the group of dominant capitalist countries the – OECD or within the Europe of the EC, and *a fortiori* not on a large scale. It is therefore not possible, objectively, to have a universal currency and thus a world central bank. The currency and the bank imply that the political problem has been solved, which is not the case.

The proposal for a world central bank reiterates the arguments advanced by Keynes in 1945. The same reasons that made the project utopian at the time are still valid today, despite the progress of economic globalization. The NIEO and the suggested 'link' between the issuance of an international currency (the SDR or Special Drawing Rights) and development were based on the same logic. The project did not lead to anything, and for good reasons. In my opinion capitalism is unable to overcome the growing contradiction between its economic management in an increasingly globalized space, and its political and social management which remain fragmented among national spaces. The alternatives are still either (worldwide) socialism or barbarism.

Nonetheless, it is necessary to respond and propose solutions. I shall be formulating some below that I believe are not utopian, because they make room for recognition of the contradiction defined above. Emerging from the perspective of the construction of a polycentric world, these proposals focus on the political and economic organization of controlled interdependencies, and the autonomy of large, unequally developed regions.

Therefore, they imply regional monetary systems and their articulation. They do not put the cart before the horse, as is the case, in my opinion, of the project for a world central bank, or even a European central bank. They are part of the logic of a very long transition, from capitalism as it is today, with its crisis, to a world socialism that cannot be achieved all at once using a magic wand, even if the wand is the creation of a world currency.

Development-funding institutions form a constellation that includes the institutions established at Bretton Woods, those established by the UN, the regional commissions and those associated with the construction of Europe. As a group, these institutions were in their heyday during the Bandung era, from 1955 to 1975, when the strategy was one of catching up through modernized, autonomous national construction, carried out in interdependence. They faced a crisis when the national bourgeois project which defined Bandung crumbled, then collapsed, while at the same time the system of capital accumulation entered into a worldwide crisis.

The World Bank

In terms of total volume of funds managed, the World Bank leaves the rest of the group far behind, with US$290 billion in transfers carried out under its authority from its inception to 1992, and a yearly volume of commitments of over $20 billion today. To this must be added some $11 billion now disbursed every year by the regional development banks. The entire United Nations system is marginal by comparison. Though it tried to set itself up as a rival of the World Bank through its own fund for agricultural development assistance created by the Food and Agriculture Organization in 1978, it was forced eventually to capitulate.

The fact remains that from 1955 to 1975, UN institutions carried out essential political and ideological functions for the Bandung Project of Third World countries. The role of the Economic Commission on Latin America (ECLA) and Raul Prebisch, a pioneer of what would eventually become the ideology of development, and the part played by UN Conference for Trade Development (UNCTAD) – an important contributor to the crystallization of the NIEO project proposed by the Third World in 1975 – were not negligible. The initiatives of these institutions probably did not have very much influence on the policies of the World Bank, but on the other hand they did have an obvious effect on the UN Development Programme (UNDP) and the specialized institutions in their heyday.

In any case, those days are gone forever, and for everyone. The ideology of development died with the demise of the Bandung Project. The time has now come for recompradorization of the peripheries through Structural Adjustment Programmes. The World Bank devotes one third of its resources to what are known as sectoral adjustment programmes, a necessary complement to the strategies instituted by the IMF under the wing of the G7 and the US administration. And yet the history of the World Bank is closely tied to the history of the expansion of the Third World's developmentalist project. As we know, in the area of European reconstruction, Washington appropriated the Bank's role directly, through its management of the famous Marshall Plan. (Nobody knows if something similar will happen with regard to Eastern Europe, after the creation of the European Bank for Recovery and Development (EBRD).) It was only later that the World Bank expanded to its full stature, under MacNamara (1968–91), while the world system was entering a crisis. Thanks to those critical minds which have taken the trouble to scrutinize the Bank's actions, we know that the Bank has never distanced itself from Washington's strategic decisions, or even from the sway of whatever fashion currently rules the White House.

The Bank has never seen itself as a public institution, competing or potentially clashing with private capital. On the contrary, it has viewed itself as an agent whose task is to support capital's penetration of the Third World through the transnationals. The projects that it has helped fund have opened up large markets to equipment suppliers. The greatest opacity prevails in this area, but these markets are known to have been not only important for transnationals, but particularly juicy. The costs of the Bank's operations have always been significantly higher than those of similar undertakings conducted by national authorities or by multilateral or bilateral aid agencies (particularly those of the Eastern-bloc countries), as evidenced by the example of the Aswan Dam, which was completed with Soviet assistance at a far lower cost than the Bank's forecasts. With cost overruns such as these, the advantages of loans at concessionary rates are not impressive.

The Bank's interventions in the mining sector were directly articulated with those of the transnationals. The Bank provided a form of insurance against the risk of nationalization, and gave indirect subsidies to mining companies by taking charge of infrastructure projects (roads, electrification, mines, railways, ports). In agriculture, the Bank has focused on destroying the autonomy of the peasant world, breaking the subsistence economy by supporting forms of credit designed to this end, and promoting the differentiation of the rural world through the green revolution. In other areas, the Bank has fulfilled equally significant functions in order to reinforce the dependent integration of Third World economies. It has systematically promoted the use of roads (as opposed to railways), opening the market to oil exports and promoting oil dependency (which aggravates the trade deficit of many countries). It has promoted the exploitation of forests for exportation, no matter how scandalous the damage to ecology, or the devastation of the country and its future. On the other hand, the Bank has been consistent in that it has contributed very little to industrialization – even to the industrialization of countries such as South Korea, which it now praises and whose achievements are the result of that country's repudiation of the Bank's precepts of opening industry to foreign capital, avoiding subsidies, etc.

Of course, the Bank's global strategy has never been concerned either before or after 1980 with the condition of the poor, as they are called today. Nor has it been concerned with the environment, whatever its rhetoric on the subject. The systematic destruction of communal lands, which it has always supported, along with deforestation, has been carried out at the expense of both ecological balance and the welfare of the majority of the popular classes. Moreover, the Bank, while pretending to be apolitical, has always shown a preference for the regimes most aligned with Washington and its allies – Mobutu, Marcos, Pinochet, Suharto or the Tontons Macoutes – without being greatly bothered by the question of democracy or by issues such as the corruption and ineffectiveness of many of its interventions under these regimes.

During a certain period of its history, the Bank had the ideological function of counteracting the 'ideology of planning' by providing a counter-ideology based on 'project analysis'. The theory was not very strong. The use of 'shadow prices' made very little sense: they could influence decisions only if they were accompanied by price controls and subsidies, which contradicted the dogma they supported. And, in fact, the 'zero' shadow price assigned to unskilled labour was used as a pretext to justify low-wage policies, in other words, to generate poverty instead of fighting it.

At the same time, the Bank has also carried out academic stylistic exercises, which, taken as a whole, are not worth much because they are always aimed at legitimizing the strategies of dominant capital. One example will suffice. In a book on the then Ivory Coast (now Côte d'Ivoire) written in 1965, I predicted 'blocking' of the system, and external indebtedness, by the year 1985. The Bank, which, of course, supported the necolonial strategy for the country, found it necessary to reply with a study costing at least fifty times more than mine, and whose perusal, today, ought to make anyone laugh.

All of the 'development-funding' institutions under consideration here, as well as the bilateral aid funds which in fact are much more important, have constituted only a fraction, not negligible, but certainly minor, of the capital market, even if we restrict ourselves to capital channelled toward distinct categories: capital seeking investment in productive activities (mining, oil and energy, agriculture, industry, transportation and communications, construction, hotels, tourism and other services); and floating capital seeking short-term financial investment.

The first of these markets has not been negligible for US, Japanese, and to a lesser extent European capital, particularly during the 1970s when 'relocation' was in full force. Europe, however, preferred to invest its wealth in the regions that were lagging behind on its own margins (Italy, Spain) rather than in areas of direct dependence. This explains the specific role played by the Lomé Convention (the EC-ACP association) in shaping the development of sub-Saharan Africa. By the support given to traditional primary exports (agriculture and mining), and its prejudice against industrialization, this convention carries a significant share of the responsibility for the African disaster and the continent's subsequent marginalization and Fourth Worldization.

The market of floating capital, which has dwarfed the first market since the 1970s, has only a marginal interest for the Third World, although it should be noted that a major fraction of the capital accumulated in many areas of Latin America, Africa, and the Middle East is collected by this market, thanks to the liberalization and globalization of financial and banking systems (which East and South-East Asia, and India, are trying to resist). On the other hand, most of this capital seeks investment by roaming from one financial metropolis to another, only rarely paying a visit to Third World financial systems. Things may be changing in this arena for a few Third World countries that might once again become attractive to capital. The World Bank and others emphasize this fact, without mentioning that most of the capital inflows in question take the form of financial investments and do not seek investment in production (this is the case for some Latin American countries). The fragility of the external balance attained under these conditions prohibits us from seeing this movement as the starting-point for sustainable development.

GATT-WTO

GATT-WTO, the regulator of trade, provides the third dimension of the system of regulation. The principles on which GATT-WTO is based are those of openness and free trade: to forbid discrimination in favour of national producers while also forbidding aggressive behaviour on the part of exporters (dumping), to reduce tariffs, and prohibit other forms of quantitative restriction (overt forms such as quotas, and unfair practices concealed by unfounded health or administrative regulations).

Supporters of GATT-WTO base their arguments on the simple yet erroneous idea that free trade favours the expansion of trade and that this expansion, in turn, favours growth. History fails to demonstrate the truth of these propositions. The expansion of trade, particularly during the postwar period, has been a consequence, rather than a cause, of the strong growth of the period (essentially derived from the subsystems of the three-part system considered above). This expansion was very rapid during the first years, despite high tariffs and other forms of protection. The subsequent crisis of the system led to the regression of world trade: the growth rate of trade fell from 7 per cent throughout the 1970s, in spite of lower tariffs and liberalization measures. Generally speaking, real history does not at all demonstrate the existence of a correlation between free trade and commercial expansion (the latter being a consequence of the former, and not the reverse), nor between periods of growth and protectionism or free trade on the part of regimes. This being said, it is true that growth encourages free trade policies whereas protectionism is often a reaction to crisis.

Advocates of free trade buttress their case by appealing to the famous theorem of neoliberal economics according to which the losses incurred by consumers as a result of tariffs are greater than the sum of the gains realized by protected producers and by the state which collects the duties. Quotas are supposed to be even worse, since they deprive the state of import duties. This demonstration, which of course implies an unreal world of perfect competition, is based, moreover, on a static analysis. History shows that the gains brought about by increases in productivity are greatly superior to those that can be obtained through competitive advantage in the best of cases. History also shows that relative prices are not determined by the market, but by the social conditions, beyond supply and demand, in which production operates. It follows that global polarization necessarily leads to, and expresses itself through, deterioration of the double factorial terms of trade, to the detriment of the peripheries, in the sense that there is more inequality in the distribution of labour remuneration than in the distribution of productivity. I would even argue that this phenomenon, intrinsic to polarized global capitalist expansion, is characteristic not only of past trade (exchanges of manufactured products from the centre for primary products from the periphery), but also of future trade between industrialized peripheries which export manufactured goods, and centres exercising their five monopolies (see pp. 3-5).

Third World governments tend to defend the basic principles of free trade. Their reasons are easily understood: for those countries that have entered into the industrial era, access to Northern markets is both possible (they are competitive) and vital (to pay for items such as imports of technology); as for the countries of the Fourth World that are still exporting primary products, they have nothing to lose and may possibly gain. This short-term vision characteristic of the comprador bourgeoisie of the periphery always overrides long-term considerations, which have never found an echo anywhere but in the radical wing of national liberation movements (what is known as the socialist wing).

But although Third World governments defend the principles of liberalism, they do so because they know that despite the rhetoric of GATT-WTO, actual practice is not in line with these principles – far from it.

In fact, a true programme of authentic liberalism on a world scale was embodied in the programme put forth by the Group of 77 and the Non-Aligned Movement in 1975 under the name of NIEO. This programme included the following points:

(1) Opening Northern markets to Southern industrial exports (the North replied by excluding textiles from the rules of GATT-WTO);

(2) Improving the terms of trade for tropical agricultural products and mining products (this would be a good way to protect the environment, but GATT-WTO has remained silent on the topic);

(3) Providing better access to international financing (GATT-WTO replied to this by liberalized banking rules that made it easier to transfer capital from the South to the North);

(4) Creating more normal conditions for technology transfers (GATT-WTO's reply was to reinforce monopolies in the name of so-called 'intellectual' property).

As we know, the NIEO Project was more or less unanimously rejected by the North.

Meanwhile, we have GATT-WTO. The first negotiating sessions – the Kennedy Round, then the Tokyo Round ending in 1979 – were devoted almost exclusively to the progressive reduction of tariffs. At the beginning of the period (1945–47) these were admittedly still almost prohibitive: 40 per cent for the average European tariff (which was fairly equally distributed) and about the same for the US tariff (which displayed a jagged outline, because it was differentiated to ensure quasi-absolute protection for threatened sectors). As I have said, these prohibitive tariffs did not seriously restrict the expansion of trade, which was occurring at an average yearly rate of 6.1 per cent – as against 4.3 per cent for the GDP – from 1953 to 1963.

During the Uruguay Round (which ended in December 1993), Western powers pursued common objectives, while attempting at the same time to reconcile some of their differences. It is important to say it clearly: the common denominator for all of the Western powers, throughout this affair, has been a marked hostility toward the Third World. The true objective of the Uruguay Round is to block the competitiveness of the industrialized

Third World, even at the expense of the holy principles of liberalism, and thus to reinforce the five monopolies of the dominant centres. In this area, as in every other area and at every other time, the double standard prevails. I would offer as evidence the following observations:

(1) Trade regulated by GATT-WTO represents only 7 per cent of world trade. Significant exclusions are textiles (this 'temporary' exclusion, under the Multifiber Agreement, has now been in place for twenty-five years!), agricultural products (including tropical oils that compete with the oils of temperate countries), mining products, etc. To offset this, developing countries are allowed reciprocally to grant each other certain preferences – a truly insignificant concession.

(2) An attack is being carried out on the means employed by Third World countries wanting to compel transnationals operating on their territories to abide by the rules of competition and to sustain national development: clauses requiring a minimal national content in production, minimal exports, etc. When transnationals are looking not for competition (through exports) but reinforcement of their monopoly position in the local market, suddenly GATT-WTO is there to help them out. The logic of the famous Trade Related Investment Measures (TRIM) inserted in the Uruguay Round is precisely this.

(3) With Trade Rights in Intellectual Property (TRIP), an offensive has been launched not to reinforce competition, but on the contrary, to strengthen the power of technological monopolies – at the expense, of course, of developing countries for whom the possibility of acquiring the technology they need in order to progress becomes even more uncertain. Will the 'trade secrets' that GATT-WTO wants to include under this category bring us back to the mercantilistic monopoly practices of 300 years ago? Even the language used to discuss the topic is not neutral. We no longer speak of knowledge as the common property of humanity, but rather of 'piracy' when someone tries to acquire it! This policy sometimes verges on the obscene: GATT-WTO, for instance, wants to forbid Third World manufacture of inexpensive pharmaceutical products, which are of vital importance, in order to protect the massive profits of monopolies in this sector.

(4) While the dominant media are busy denouncing corruption, GATT-WTO wants to prohibit Third World countries from employing

inspectors to monitor the prices charged by Western exporters – prices which provide an ideal opportunity for corruption and tax evasion through illegal transfers of capital.

(5) The offensive in favour of opening markets to the activities of Western banks and insurance companies is intended to accelerate the transfer of capital from South to North. Asia is opposed to this. How long will it be able to resist?

GATT-WTO's claim to defend 'fair competition' is far from justified. It is, in fact, an organization entirely subservient to the transnationals. As we know, it is the most opaque institution imaginable, meeting in secret in the shadow of the international Chamber of Commerce (the club of the biggest transnationals). Not surprisingly, then, GATT-WTO is utterly oblivious to issues of sustainable development, which are confined to debates in other forums. It is equally oblivious to the environment, protesting, at the expense of the future, against any regulation of the mining industry. The deregulation recommended by GATT-WTO is simply intended to benefit transnational monopolies by reducing to zero the space in which states (and particularly Third World states) can exercise management.

Compared with GATT-WTO's common front against the Third World, divergences between the major Western powers within GATT-WTO, when restored to their true perspective, do not have the importance attributed to them by the dominant media (which have remained silent on other issues). Many of these conflicts, indeed, are settled by 'amicable arrangements' between competing monopolists who practise market-sharing or 'voluntary restrictions' of exports, in flat contradiction to the dogma of liberalism. However, other conflicts have provided the United States with opportunities to express its arrogance openly:

(1) The conflict between the United States, the EC, and Japan over agricultural subsidies (covered by what is known as the Blair House agreement) is the best known. It is a fact that the countries of the EC are now self-sufficient in food, and have even become food exporters, by delinking their prices from those of the world market – a practice forbidden to the Third World countries by the EC. It is equally true that Japan (and Korea) would like to maintain their food self-sufficiency by protecting their rice producers. However, US subsidies to agriculture existed long before the Common Agricultural Policy of the EC.

(2) Conflicts over what are referred to as 'subsidized' sectors, such as

aeronautics, focus on overt subsidies given to civil aviation, while ignoring the mammoth disguised subsidies through which military programmes support the US aeronautics industry.

(3) In the area of technology, the United States always reserves the right to protect its own for reasons of 'security', but it always requires that other countries be open to its technological spying. Resistance in this area is deemed unacceptable, and gives rise to US threats of reprisal under the famous Super 301 and 301 special clauses.

However, since GATT-WTO directly represents transnationals and not states, conflicts in these areas do not oppose states as much as they appear to. In most cases opinion is divided within each country aligned behind the particular interests that support or oppose the conflicting positions within GATT-WTO.

Globalization: The Necessity of International Economic Management

The globalization of the capitalist system is certainly nothing new, but it has undeniably taken a qualitative step forward during the most recent period. Moreover, this deepening economic interdependence between nations occurs at a time when there is a crisis of accumulation, and the postwar boom has given way to stagnation. This new situation has been met by a response shaped by the dominant interests of capital. Will this response be sustained? Will it allow the crisis to be managed correctly, that is, without aggravating the dangers of chaos and collapse? Will it go further and prepare the ground for a resumption of growth?

Criticism of the policies carried out by the Bretton Woods institutions cannot be separated from the answers given to these questions. In the same way, the proposals for alternative solutions to replace these policies cannot be separated from the overall social and political perspective in which the vision of 'actually existing capitalism' is located.

The advance of globalization has not been confined to trade. (A considerable part – approximately one third – of the industrial and agricultural output of the advanced capitalist countries is now exchanged on the world market.) It also affects productive systems (autocentric national systems are progressively dismantled to be reconstituted as part of an integrated global productive system), technology (specific national technologies make way for universal technologies), financial markets, and many other aspects of social life. A simultaneous phenomenon is the integration of Third World countries that have embarked on industrialization. (I attribute this transformation to the victory of national liberation movements after the Second World War and the support provided to the Bandung Project by the Eastern-bloc countries, and not at all to the logic of capitalist expansion having modified the terms of the international division of labour and eroded the classic forms of the centre/periphery polarization to begin replacing these soon-to-be-obsolete forms with the five monopolies mentioned above.)

Of course, by definition, the new globalization erodes the efficiency of economic management by national states. However, it does not abolish their existence. Thus, it produces a new contradiction which, in my opinion, is insurmountable under capitalism. The reason for this is that capitalism is more than just an economic system; its economy is inconceivable without a social and political dimension, which implies a state. Until recently, the expansion of capitalism was founded on the coincidence between the space in which the reproduction of accumulation was determined and the space of its political and social management: the space of the central national state shaped the structure of the international system. Now, however, we have entered a new era characterized by a separation between the globalized space of capitalism's economic management and the national spaces of its political and social management.

Under these conditions, the logic of the interests of dominant capital would require that priority be given to globalized economic management, at the expense of the functions of the national state. This logic is displayed in the full-scale anti-state discourse of the dominant media calling for elimination of the state's social interventions, massive privatization, etc. These fallacious arguments are easily refuted. Privatization of social services is expensive and inefficient; health care in the United States, for example, costs twice as much as in Europe, and is of inferior quality. However, it is highly profitable (to US insurance companies). Privatization replaces public bureaucracies, which might be subject to some form of democratic control, with irresponsible and opaque private bureaucracies. In most Third World countries, the public sector has not only carried out pioneering tasks which were beyond the capacity of the local or foreign private sector but, in some cases, through the substitution of public monopolies for private ones, has, for example, helped finance accumulation and correct income distribution. Of course, the social content of nationalization under the Bandung (bourgeois national) Project determined the limits of this nationalization. The income produced was channelled in the first place toward the expansion of the new middle classes rather than the popular classes, and management was sometimes deficient, either for objective reasons (lack of the resources necessary to carry out modernization in time), political and social reasons (the deficit of the public sector financed the expansion of a parasitical private sector), or reasons of political management (extending to corruption). But private capitalism is certainly not any better, socially speaking, and is not even assuredly more efficient. (Studies have shown that public sector profitability in the major industrialized countries of Asia and Latin America was higher, on the average, than the profitability of comparable private sectors in the West.) In fact, then, the attack against the state contradicts the rhetoric being produced at the same time in favour of democracy, transparency and efficiency. Unfortunately, a great many NGOs have adopted this position, contributing to the anti-state discourse, without realizing that the results of capital's offensive in this area are always catastrophic for the popular classes.

It has rarely been noted that privatization plays an important part in management of the crisis, providing outlets for the excess capital characteristic of the crisis. In my opinion, this is one of the major reasons for the operation. But at what price? Capital thus invested contributes nothing to the development of the productive system (and thus fails to reduce unemployment). Returns obtained by capital under these conditions aggravate inequality in the state's subsequent capacity to intervene so as to palliate the negative effects of globalization.

The project of reducing management of the system to regulation by the world market is, therefore, truly utopian. As Kostas Vergopoulos has pointed out, national coherence is regressing, but it is not being replaced by worldwide coherence, which remains elusive. This is not surprising, for such coherence would require a world state, or, at least, a political system as effective at the global level as the national state has been at its level. International economic institutions do not fill the void. As we have seen, they are merely the instruments of capital's management of the market. The UN, now devalued, is not progressing toward the construction of a world political system; on the contrary, it is losing ground in this area. Recognizing this failure, Vergopoulos expresses some justified reservations about the reality of 'globalization'. He observes that despite the globalization of markets, national macro-economic structures are still highly important determinants. 'Competition' between firms is in fact competition between national units. He writes: 'Globalized firms do exist, but national economic systems are not globalized yet'. Under these conditions, globalization increases disparities and incoherences. Therefore, it remains fragile. The system under these conditions may be brought to a point where it explodes, or it may evolve toward competitive regionalization, as we will see below.

Globalization proceeds against a backdrop of stagnation. Is it the cause of this stagnation? I would provide an answer formulated in dialectical and discriminating terms: stagnation is not a direct product of globalization, but capitalistic globalization is responsible for the erosion of the three subsystems that formed the basis of postwar growth (the national welfare state in the West, the national bourgeois project of Bandung in the Third World, and Sovietism in the Eastern bloc). Furthermore, stagnation is perpetuated and aggravated by the policies employed by dominant capital to manage the crisis.

Stagnation (which has now characterized the system for twenty-five years) naturally gives rise to a gigantic surplus of capital which finds no outlet in productive investment. Under these conditions, the response of dominant capital to the situation is perfectly logical: priority is given to the management of this mass of floating capital. This management requires maximum worldwide financial openness and high interest rates. At the same time, the system allows the United States to maintain its negative position as it finances its deficit by draining the mass of floating capital; this is the only way for it to maintain its hegemony (by imposing the dollar as the international currency by default, and by sustaining an extremely high level of military spending). On the other hand, the system undoubtedly has the following flaws: (i) it fails to provide stable exchange rates, even between the major currencies (dollar, yen, mark, and, as a secondary consideration, pound and franc), thus distorting the rules of international competition; (ii) it leads to a spiral of worldwide stagnation, making unemployment a permanent feature of Western societies; and (iii) it blocks the possibility of pursuing the development of many peripheral regions. As far as the first of these flaws is concerned, the major decisional centres (particularly the G7) are looking for ways to correct it or adjust to it. However, the stagnation and devastation caused by crisis-management policies, embodied in the other two points, are not really an object of concern for dominant capital. Unemployment is a problem for the jobless, not for capitalists. And if unemployment is needed to maintain capital profitability, then long live unemployment! Nor is development of the periphery a goal of capital's strategies. On the contrary. These strategies involve adapting to, profiting by, in the most literal sense, the growth or stagnation of peripheries, and since there are no attractive investments in this situation, dominant capital finds its profit in managing the Third World debt. Finding a solution to the problem is not on the agenda, simply because this is not in capital's interest.

We may now return to the assessment of strategies conducted before the crisis. Beginning in 1945, the welfare state, which until then existed only in embryonic form, was systematically supported, not particularly by the Bretton Woods institutions (their role here was more than modest), but by the states, that is, the political systems of the Western powers. Was this because the light of Keynesianism had finally illuminated their darkness?

Was it because dominant capital had converted to the utility of the social sphere? Not at all. It was because the 'threat' of communism existed at this time. Hegemonic political blocs in the West had to rise to the challenge, and so they did. In the same way, development in the Third World was not produced by the conversion of Western élites to anticolonialism; it was imposed by the success of national liberation movements, movements which benefited from the support of the Eastern-bloc countries. The disintegration of Sovietism (the last element of our three-part system) modified social relations, in the West and in the Third World, to the benefit of dominant capital. Capital reverted swiftly to its original nature, seizing the opportunity to break the workers' movements in the West (through unemployment) and the national liberation movement in the Third World (by dismantling development and instituting recompradorization). The discourse of the powerful bemoaning unemployment and poverty – as if these phenomena were not the result of their policies – is pure hypocrisy.

International economic institutions do not bear direct, primary responsibility for this state of affairs. They are merely instruments. Yesterday, they were set to serve the postwar boom in Europe and Japan (by guaranteeing exchange-rate stability while in-depth actions were undertaken as part of the Marshall Plan and European-construction), and development in the Third World (by making it swerve to the right, which led it to become exhausted more quickly). Today they are ready to serve the system adopted to manage the crisis.

The internationalization of banks plays an important part in the analysis of crisis management that I am suggesting. But floating exchange rates and the continuous growth of the mass of free capital provided banks with the opportunity for fruitful participation in the financial speculation to manage the crisis. At the same time, the internationalization of banks (and insurance companies) allowed the savings of the South to be drained by the North's speculative financial market. Of course, all of this may be judged scandalous, and there is every reason to assert and reassert that private capital cannot replace central banks in their role, thus annihilating that role, and that these functions must be public. But however scandalous these practices may be, they are not absurd.

We have been living with floating exchange rates for over twenty years now. This experience disproves completely the theoretical neoclassical discourse that was developed to legitimize their establishment. Experience shows there is no natural equilibrium of exchange rates, but that rates determine structural adjustments which are always, or nearly always, asymmetrical, and which either work or fail to work. Supposedly automatic capital flows which offset balance-of-payments imbalances, and are chiefly made up of major flows of productive investment, exist only in the imagination of university professors. On the contrary, speculative flows, which constitute the majority, confer on exchange rates a volatility which robs them of all rationality. Not only does this volatility lead to grave macro-economic disorders (destruction of the productive base in the case of overvaluation, parasitical development of export activities that are unsustainable in the long term in the case of undervaluation), but it also perpetuates micro-economic inefficiencies. When the value of the dollar in relation to other currencies has doubled or halved, each time within the space of a few months, what economic calculation – except the speculative type – can be made on this basis? How can tariffs be effective when facing the relative price variations determined by such fluctuations in the exchange rate?

Nevertheless, floating exchange rates permit massive growth of the 'need for liquidities', thus providing an outlet for idle capital generated by the crisis. According to the theory, floating exchange rates were supposed to release central banks from the problem of having to manage reserves in whatever constituted the international standard. The theory forgot that insecurity provoked by the volatility of exchange rates would force all agents operating in external markets to constitute significant private reserves to deal with unpredictable fluctuations. As a consequence, these reserve liquidities had to be provided with earnings, hence the necessity for high interest rates.

In this way, floating exchange rates also bear part of the responsibility for persisting stagnation. Concern for equilibrium of the balance of payments, which is permanently threatened by speculative capital movements, leads to the ascendancy of a logic that systematically gives priority to anti-inflation policies and exports, even if this obviously requires a contraction of internal demand. Perverse competition, and a generalized deflationist spiral, are the outcome. The G7 has repeatedly attempted to put some order in the exchange rates of the dollar, yen, and mark. In view of current reality, we can say only that it has not been very successful.

And yet, relative stability of exchange rates has been achieved within the European community. The reason is that the EC's internal structural complementarities allow a certain harmonization of the remuneration of production factors, which is reinforced by flows of productive investments (from the European centres to its peripheries). The EC also represents a zone of political security and solidarity, and as such can offer its members a certain monetary stability in their mutual relationships. However, this stability is fragile, precisely because the same system cannot be extended as a whole to Europe, the United States, and Japan. A conflict of mercantile interests, which is not tempered at this level by group solidarities, thus threatens the European partners, but it threatens each of them to a specific and different degree. Europe could only answer this challenge by withdrawing more into itself. Attitudes toward this option diverge, since 'strong' countries (Germany) necessarily differ from the others in preferring openness.

Under the system adopted to manage crisis, the United States is still allowed not to worry about its deficit. This deficit is large enough to absorb all of the surpluses of the other developed regions (for the 1980-89 decade the US deficit was US$931 billion, while surpluses stood at $533 billion for Japan, $396 billion for Germany, and $103 billion for the tigers of eastern Asia), and it has drained the international market of capital that would otherwise have been available for other regions of the world. Under these conditions, the hegemony of the United States may certainly be described as a 'false hegemony'. Great Britain, the hegemonic power in the nineteenth century, had a structural surplus: 50 per cent of its gross capital formation was invested abroad between 1870 and 1914, thus providing for the structural adjustment of others. This is not at all the case of the United States today; on the contrary, the country's deficit makes structural adjustment impossible for it.

Thus, the system is satisfied with unilateral structural adjustment on the part of the weakest partners (the Third World), at the expense of their development. At the same time, as part of the array of measures implemented to this effect, systematically undervalued exchange rates are imposed on Third World countries. Having finally discovered this obvious fact, which ensures that the rhetoric on the 'truth of prices' supposedly revealed by the market is completely meaningless, the IMF has undertaken to revise the estimated GDP of these countries upward, recalculating it on the basis of fictional exchange rates based on equality of purchasing power. This measure is purely symbolic and even demagogic, since decisions are not made on the basis of these fictional rates but on the basis of real rates, which the IMF, of course, does not intend to revise. In extreme cases – but these are becoming more and more numerous – the monetary aspect of the imposed adjustment leads to 'dollarization'. Not only as a reserve instrument, but even as a unit of measurement and an exchange medium, the national currency gives way to the dollar, of which imports are financed by external borrowing. The cycle is now complete, the crisis management system having succeeded in providing a new outlet for floating capital in search of investment.

The G7 was constituted to coordinate management of the crisis at the level of the major capitalist powers. We have already mentioned the fact that it has met with very limited success in the area of exchange stabilization. As manager of the crisis, the G7 is 'a world executive with no overall project for the world'. It was content to set up the principles of unilateral adjustment by the periphery in 1976, to organize the recycling of oil dollars in 1980 to the benefit of the speculative financial sphere and then to encourage the fall in the prices of raw materials (the major reason for the Gulf War), to organize the rescheduling of the debt in 1982 (but not to create the conditions that would solve the problem), and in 1992 to include Russia and the countries of Eastern Europe in strategies of unilateral adjustment.

So the strategy is intended to manage the crisis rather than look for ways to resolve it. In this context, even the existence of the debt is perfectly functional, and to solve this problem would in fact be counterproductive from the system's point of view. This is why all of the measures taken, measures which are sometimes presented, demagogically, as solutions, have merely made the situation worse. The debt grew from US$900 billion in 1982 to $1,500 trillion, of which half was expended on interest.

Is this type of management strong enough to last? This is the real question. The argument that it cannot last because it does not provide a way out of the tunnel of stagnation is not valid, because the goal is not to resolve the crisis but to manage it. If we confine ourselves to the analysis of economic and financial mechanisms, I would say that this management can indeed be pursued successfully, maintaining the world in a state of stagnation. For countries at the periphery, this stagnation leads to a grave regressive involution of which the Fourth Worldization of Africa is simply the most extreme example. Crisis management seeks to encourage exports from each country of the centre (thus exacerbating trade conflicts between these countries), to deprive Third World countries of the same possibility (by halting industrial relocation in order to lessen the growth of unemployment at the centre). Here again, one is reminded of the order established at Versailles in 1919: make Germany pay, but don't let it export goods! In another striking analogy documented in Walter Russell Mead's study, police forces are busy hunting down new emigrants created by regression in the Third World. Finally, crisis management is a strategy that will exacerbate conflicts between developed countries (not only between the United States, Japan and the EC, and even within the EC itself, whose existence is threatened), and that leads developed countries to consider no other means than force (and war) in their relations with the Third World. For this reason, US (military) hegemony remains indispensable, obliging European and Japanese partners to make the concessions required by the United States, and thus turning their conflicts back into the EC. Will the 'regionalizations' brought about by the dynamic of these conflicts, almost spontaneously (but in as much as they are sustained by adequate options) become the system's 'way out' of an impossible globalization? There are indeed indicators pointing in this direction: the creation of the North American Free Trade Association, (NAFTA) in North America (though NAFTA breaks Mexico in two by separating its Texan north from its

Guatemalan south, as the Chiapas revolt has just confirmed, increasing the fragility of Washington's project, which is supported by the Mexican comprador bourgeoisie); the fact that the EC already carries out two thirds of its trade through its internal exchange, and that this internal exchange is increasing, while the community's exports to the outside world have been declining since 1985 (but will this last?); the fact that, even without any formal common institution, the countries of eastern Asia (Japan, Korea, China, South-East Asia) carry out two thirds of their trade through internal exchange (but the United States is exerting very strong pressure to break these complementarities; this is the most important reason for the United States' pursuit of growth in this part of the world, and the project of an 'Asia-Pacific zone' evoked by Clinton is part of the same intention).

Thus, if the system adopted to manage the crisis cannot survive in the long term, this is due not to the absurdity of its underlying economic and monetary policies, but to the aggravation of social and political conflicts which it cannot avoid. Here we return to the thesis I am defending: the idea that management through the market is utopian, that the real management of capitalism requires 'market plus state', that the conflict between globalized economic space and the fragmentation of spaces for political and social management is unbearable, and that it must lead to a renewal of nationalisms and social struggles, which will challenge the utopian globalization pursued during the crisis.

But will this challenge lead to an even more marked general regression or to a new general period of economic growth? I believe that discussion of the alternatives to the current system should focus on this question.

Reforming Bretton Woods

It is not possible to review all of the proposals put forth in recent years for reform of the Bretton Woods institutions. They are too numerous; moreover they are derived from theoretical and political perspectives that are extremely diverse. I will, therefore, confine myself to a small sample of proposals made from a resolutely progressive point of view – that is, they start from the objective of a renewed development throughout the world, and especially in the Third World; they give this development a popular content (elimination of poverty, expansion of social services, reduction of inequalities); and they allow unity to be re-established between the economic and the political sphere (which means, among other things, allowing democracy to take root among peoples).

I certainly have a great deal of sympathy for these proposals – not only for the general spirit animating the solutions advanced, but even, in many cases, for the detail of the reforms suggested at three levels of necessary action: local, national and global. To support transformations of attitudes and organization of responsibility at the base, to enable people at this level to become genuine agents of economic initiative and thus create a link between the economic sphere and political, social and cultural life, to free them from the status which capitalism confers on them of reducing workers to their labour-power and citizens to consumers – these are, without a doubt, essential conditions for better development. However, struggles carried on in this perspective must be supported by adequate policies at the three levels. At the national level, which in my view remains the crucial link simply because of the existence of a political organization that we will be experiencing for a long time yet, what I call delinking – not autarky, but the subordination of outside relations to the logic of internal development and not the reverse – is unavoidable. It remains necessary to define its exact contours, and this can be done only on the concrete basis of situations that vary greatly from one country to another. It is therefore a matter of forcing the world system to adapt: not only of imposing a vision of adjustment within stagnation, but also of replacing the concept of unilateral adjustment (of the weakest to the strongest) by the concept of mutual adjustment. These national policies in turn would require, to be sufficiently effective, not only the reconstruction of solidarity and mutual support between countries at the periphery (particularly through the construction of regional unions), but also, most probably, transformations in the economic and political organization of the world system.

In this last area, there is no lack of ideas. The most radical proposals call for a return to Keynesianism, this time on a world scale: a redistribution of income to the benefit of Third World peoples and workers in every region of the world (a 'megaeconomic stimulation', as Walter Russell Mead says). According to their advocates, these proposals imply major reforms affecting the international economic institutions:

(1)   The transformation of the IMF into a genuine world central bank with the power of issuing a real currency (similar to the SDRs) that would replace the dollar standard, ensure a certain stability of exchange rates, and provide developing countries with the liquidities needed for 'adjustment within growth' (these proposals resemble those made by UNCED some twenty years ago to create a link between issuance of an international currency and the needs of developing countries).

(2)   The transformation of the World Bank into a fund that would collect surpluses (from countries such as Japan and Germany) and

lend them not to the United States, but to the Third World. This operation, intended to trigger growth in developing countries, would simultaneously force the United States to reduce its deficit. It is hoped that this reduction would not be obtained through US neoprotectionism associated with an aggressive exports policy. But how else would it happen?

(3) The creation of a genuine international trade organization (ITO). In this area, in general, the principle of free trade as advocated by GATT-WTO is not questioned. The ITO might even be bolder than GATT-WTO, which is always forced to manoeuvre in a context of compromise, and might succeed in imposing out-and-out multilateralism. As a counterpart to the benefits that developing countries would receive from the genuine opening of Northern markets, they would be asked to make concessions (of the TRIM and TRIP type) in the area of services. The experience of the EC, which has actually succeeded in liberalizing and multilateralizing intra-European trade while excluding unbridled competition (for example, by imposing standards of respect for the environment and social protection), is often mentioned in this respect. It is also argued that the ITO would temper the negative aspects of the creation of regional units (for example, EC, NAFTA) by preventing them from becoming fortresses, protected within and aggressive without. The ITO would have other objectives such as the stabilization (or revalorization) of raw materials.

(4) Consideration of environmental issues might become an internalized feature of the World Bank's loan system. One might take this even further by setting up a world tax on energy, non-renewable resources, etc., that would increase the resources available to the Bank (or the fund that would take its place), allowing it to subsidize respect for environmental concerns in poor countries.

(5) Reform of the economic institutions would be accompanied by a heightened political role for the United Nations. Development having been revived by the means we have described, the project of making it the basis for the progress of political and social democracy could become more than a pious wish. Development aid, multilateralized within this framework, might not only be conditional on respect for individual rights and political democracy, but also support progressive social policies (making sure that wage increases parallel increases in productivity, providing for a more

equal distribution of income, etc.). In the same way, the national political dimension of globalized development, coordinated in this way, would allow for the respect of legitimate interests. For example, food self-sufficiency (Walter Russell Mead has studied the case of Japan's protection of its rice producers) would be accepted, but it would be offset by a tax paid to the world community by the country benefiting from the protectionist measures. The tax would be collected by a world development fund which would be the major lending institution for Third World countries.

In my opinion, this is a very fine project for reform of the world economic and political system. It proceeds from a central idea that strikes me as incontrovertible: that development can only be revived by a redistribution of income both at the global level (in favour of the peripheries) and at the social level (within centres and peripheries, in favour of workers and the popular classes), and that world trade and capital movements must be subordinated to the logic of this 'demand-side approach to trade', as Walter Russell Mead calls it.

Yet it must be recognized that reforms of this scope clash with the interests of dominant capital, because redistribution reduces profit margins in the short term, even though, in the longer term, it produces more than recovery – a genuine period of new growth that might open perspectives for profitable productive investments. For capitalism is a system based on giving priority to short-term considerations over long-term requirements which, in case of necessity, must be imposed by state intervention. I have already said that it was the fear of communism and the radicalization of the national liberation movements of the peripheries that gave rise to the Keynesian policies and development support of the postwar period.

The project is thus a kind of rediscovery of the fact that a different social order – socialism, to call it by its name – is objectively necessary and must be worldwide. It strikes me as evident that the deployment of this project demands deep political changes in every part of the world, the replacement of existing hegemonic social alliances (based on the domination of comprador capitalism in the peripheries of the South and now the East) with different social alliances based on the hegemony of labour and the popular classes. This is the only way in which it is possible to establish the dominance of use values over exchange values, and the integration of long-term requirements (the environment). At the same time, the project requires a different world political order from the one that prevails currently, an order based on the democratization of all societies and the articulation of their interdependence with mutual respect for diversity.

Advances in these directions are necessary and possible. But I use the word advances advisedly, for realization of the project as a whole is a long-term affair, the secular 'transition' from globalized capitalism to world socialism. Along with the ideological combat that must be fought over the vision of the ultimate objective (as it is conceived, for example, in the project we have described), strategies must also be defined for each step of the way.

Returning to the project, therefore, I have made it the object of a constructive critique which can be summarized in the following points:

(1) Many of the analyses underlying the reformist arguments are too much inclined to mix value judgements (the current system is 'bad') with explanations of the reasons motivating the decisions of the dominant powers. As I have said, the crisis management system that has been implemented is not absurd: it obeys the logic of dominant interests. Along with Sweezy and Magdoff, I believe that globalization as it is practised today is not a force imposing itself on humanity from the outside, but fulfils goals that are those of capital.

(2) I do not believe that transforming the IMF into a world central bank, and the World Bank into a fund for development, ought to be the objectives for the immediate future in this long transition to world socialism. Before reaching this point, it is necessary to construct a polycentric world on both the economic and the political levels; I have written elsewhere on some of the guiding principles of such a world. To believe it is possible to go any faster is to imagine that the basic political problem is solved, that the contradiction between economic globalization and the fragmentation of political spaces is already surmounted. But this can only occur at the end of a long transition; it cannot be a condition for undertaking reforms. I am afraid that by setting the bar too high we are condemning ourselves to failure, and in so doing, there is a risk that we will encourage despair and the spread of the 'TINA syndrome' ('there is no alternative' – no alternative of course, but to submit to the logic of dominant capital).

(3) Because the status of globalization has not always been clearly defined (is it a determining objective force, or one tendency among others?) certain elements of the reform project outlined above strike me as doubtful. For example, I do not believe in the virtues of free trade (or in the concessions required of the periphery on its account). I prefer the vision of the authors of *The New Protectionism* to that of the advocates of a genuine free trade system.

The priorities for action that I am suggesting are therefore different from those outlined in the project under consideration. I emphasize actions to be undertaken in the following major directions:

(1) Constructing Third World regions organized to face the five monopolies of dominant capitalism, and therefore capable of limiting their negative effects from the point of view of ongoing global polarization.

(2) Reviving the European Left and the construction of Europe, enriched by a progressive social content representing an advance, in this region, towards a hegemony of labour, integrating Eastern Europe and the former USSR into this project.

(3) Reviewing the financial and commercial relations between Europe, Japan and the United States in a direction that would permit a relative stabilization of exchange rates and force the United States to give up its structural deficit; reorganization of trade relations in this perspective.

(4) Reconstructing the UN system in order to make it the locus of political and economic negotiations to organize the articulation of commercial and financial interdependence between the major regions of the world; opening negotiations on disarmament; taking the first steps toward the creation of a world taxation system organized around objectives of protecting the environment and natural resources.

(5) Reforming the IMF as an expression of these regional/world interdependencies, and not implying its immediate transformation into a world bank.

In conclusion, I will say once again that the realism of this project is based on an understanding of history that does not accept the idea that historical laws precede history itself. What appear as objective forces (such as globalization) are only the products of a logic specific to a given system (in this case, capitalism), forms which are contradicted by the social interests of the forces that struggle against their realization. The real result of this conflict determines a configuration of subsystems expressed in a certain manner, depending on social relations of power and the outcome of struggle – thus a configuration which is permanently evolving of its own accord. The strategy of creating a world socialism necessary to avoid barbarism focuses on defining the paths most likely to lead to evolution in the direction of this objective.

References

Baran, Paul and Paul Sweezy, *Monopoly Capital*, New York, 1966

Lang, Tim and Colin Hines, *The New Protectionism, Protecting the Future Against Free Trade*, Earthscan Pub. Ltd., London, 1993

Mead, Walter Russell, 'American Economic Policy in the Antemillenial Era', mimeographed paper presented to preparatory conference on '50 years is enough', Washington, USA, March 1995

Sweezy, Paul, *The Theory of Capitalist Development*, Dennis Dobson, London, 1946

Sweezy, Paul and Harry Magdoff, 'Globalization – To What End?', Monthly Review, Vol. 43, No. 9 (February 1992), pp. 1-18; No. 10 (March 1992), pp. 1-19

Vergopoulos, Kostas, Le Nouveau Systeme Monde, Actuel-Marx, PUF, Paris, 1994

CHAPTER 3

Reforming International Monetary Management of the Crisis

Background

The present international monetary and financial system, put together at the end of the Second World War and managed by the IMF, is no longer functional. It should not surprise us that the long postwar period that began in 1945 eventually came to an end in 1990, or that the world system which will evidently succeed it will be qualitatively different from what we have known for nearly half a century.

I have elsewhere defined the postwar cycle as a long path of ascent built on a foundation consisting of three pillars, partly in conflict but partly complementary: (i) in the West, social-democracy and Fordist accumulation regulated by Keynesian national policies – open to the world market, to be sure, but consistent nonetheless with a coherence between accumulation and the historic capital/labour compromise; (ii) modernization and industrialization in the newly-independent peripheries, managed by what I have designated as the Bandung Project, a national bourgeois project of catching up in a context of circumscribed independence; (iii) the Soviet project, catching up with the West by means of an accumulation strategy much like that of historical capitalism, free nonetheless of the constraints of the capitalist world system and managed on the level of the national or multinational state by means of state ownership and the centralization of political and economic power in the hands of a new bourgeoisie-in-formation, the nomenclature of the communist parties.

This tripolar system constituted the basis of a (generally) strong economic expansion in each of the three regions. In this context, these projects and even their success were from the beginning ideological illusions which operated with the force of fixed beliefs. In the West, one believed that steady growth was already an established fact. In the Third World one believed that nation-building would ultimately resolve the problems of underdevelopment. In the countries of the East one believed in socialism.

The forceful return of the business crisis that marks the end of this phase of expansion is the joint product of the three models that made up the system during the postwar years. It has plunged all of the regions of the planet into a profound and lasting structural crisis, and no indicators seem to detect light at the end of the tunnel, either for the West, the East, or the South.

The world monetary system has always corresponded strictly to the organizing structures of the world order: to each phase of the history of capitalism there has been a particular monetary counterpart. That of the postwar period corresponded perfectly to the hegemony of the United States. It was one of the instruments that enforced US hegemony over its allies and the countries of the Third World, while the countries that were called socialist excluded themselves by delinking from it.

In the debates at Bretton Woods in 1945 two positions were advanced. Keynes, in proposing the creation of a world central bank capable of issuing international money, defended the position of the declining imperial nations, Great Britain in particular. The value of the international currency, tied to a market basket of 'key currencies', presupposed a stable compromise between the new hegemony of the United States and its subaltern allies. The Soviet Union and its allies were excluded from that compromise. The United States had imposed this solution, making the dollar the only world currency, equivalent to gold by virtue of a fixed dollar–gold exchange-rate. The system of fixed exchange rates permitted devaluation of currencies relative to the US dollar in proportion to their nations' decline relative to the irresistible hegemony of the United States.

As soon as US hegemony began to decline, beginning with the suspension of the convertibility of the dollar in 1971, the whole system was called into question. Nonetheless, the ongoing decline of the United States did not by itself initiate a reform of the monetary system, just as the decline of Great Britain beginning in the 1880s did not dethrone sterling until 1931. If one were now to try to maintain the dollar standard, the monetary system would move fatally toward a disorderly breakup like that of the period of 1930–45.

Flexible Exchange Rates are No Solution

The system of flexible exchange rates adopted in 1971 is not a real solution. It merely acknowledges the existence of disorder. Moreover, this system has accentuated exchange rate fluctuations that have no basis in changes at the level of production: the weak dollar in the seventies, dropping at least to the level of four French francs; the strong Reagan dollar during the eighties, climbing to the level of ten francs and then dropping again.

I grant that hegemony always presents multiple faces and operates at diverse and complementary levels. Hegemony is not reducible to 'economic efficiency', to 'competitiveness' on the world market, even if that is its ultimate basis, and monetary dominance is not the only instrument by which it is asserted. The military role of the United States, policeman of the world system, is equally important. From now on this role will be strengthened by the collapse of the Soviet Union, which formerly imposed limits on the intervention of the United States in the Third World.

Today one often hears the claim that military hegemony is not long-lasting, because it costs too much and American society is not disposed to assume the cost, as the election of Clinton has demonstrated. I have some reservations about this thesis for at least two reasons. The first is that a serious reduction in US military expenditure would plunge the country into an economic crisis at least as serious as that of the 1930s. Along with Sweezy and Magdoff, I am one who considers that capitalism is a social formation with a permanent tendency to overproduce, in which the 'crisis' is the normal state of affairs and prosperity has to be explained by recourse to special factors. Thus, the United States could only recover from the crisis of the 1930s through over-arming itself during the Second World War and the years that followed. Today the US economy is monstrously deformed: almost a third of economic activity depends directly or indirectly on the military complex, a proportion reached in the Soviet Union only during the epoch of Brezhnev. The second is that military hegemony pays, precisely through the privilege that the dollar as a world currency confers. Therefore, for Washington to accept a reduction in its role on the world's stage, to see a sharing of responsibilities with Europe and Japan, would precipitate a reform of the international monetary system, the loss of privilege for the dollar, and therefore, far from permitting economies, would dry up the favourable flow of capital.

The complex situation of our crisis is therefore to be long-lasting. That is why the pronouncements of the powers have come to centre on the development of the crisis and not on getting out of it. For example, it is not a question of reducing unemployment in the West but of 'living with it'. The talk is of 'an economy with two speeds', and so forth. According to this logic the most powerful partners seek to transfer the maximum possible burden of the crisis to the weakest partners – the peripheries of the South and now the East – in order to play down its consequences at home and to avoid its becoming dramatic, even if such a tactic does not help to find a solution to the crisis. From this perspective the management of the crisis preserves the existing international monetary system for a while longer, at least, although its days are numbered. But such preservation of a bygone system in the face of winds and storms runs the risk of its collapse, as in 1930, when the sterling standard gave way to uncoordinated rivalries that were harbingers of war.

Reform Proposals Emanating from the Mainstream

That being the case, it is useful to examine the alternative proposals offered by the specialists, which are sometimes the objects of diplomatic consideration.

These proposals are all prefaced with the observation, correct and important, that globalization has deepened in the postwar years, to the point of having passed over into a qualitatively new stage. The national production systems, historical constructs of the national bourgeois states that have become the centres of world capitalism, have been progressively dismantled in favour of a global production system. The industrialization of the peripheries has integrated them into this qualitatively new system.

The logical conclusion that one can draw from this observation is that world capitalism needs a world organization on all levels, on the monetary level certainly, but also on the political level. It needs a world central bank (and therefore a new world money issued by the bank), or if not it needs a world state, or at least some sort of effective world political organization.

I would say of this logic that it takes seriously the liberal argument: the world market ought to evolve towards integration at all levels, that is to say, to abolish all boundaries to the movement of merchandise and services, of capital and of labour power, to open itself to the migration of people on a par with the movements of products and capital. This is the sense of the building of a 'world state'.

But right away we see that the project, and therefore the propositions that are embodied in its logic, particularly the management of a world money, are utopian. Our real world is and will for a long time remain founded on a grand contradiction between the globalization of the economy, based on a truncated market system which includes trading in commodities and capital but excludes migration of labour power, and the persistence of the national state as the structure for the regulation of politics and social life. This contradiction, which produced and reproduces the polarization of the world, will be fatal for capitalism.

We may now return to the proposals that have been offered concerning the world monetary system. They are three in number:

(1) The first is a return to gold, which alone can stand against the currents of the whirlpool. I exclude this possibility, but not because capitalism has finally liberated itself from this old fetish; on the contrary, capitalism is and will remain fundamentally fetishistic. I exclude it because the regulation of the monetary system by means of merchandise money whose production is largely independent of other economic considerations corresponds to the mode of regulation of 'competitive', pre-monopolistic capitalism. The regulation of credit is the only alternative to this now-dead mode of regulation.

(2) The second is the creation of a world central bank, without which there could not concurrently be put in place a world political institution with analogous power. This was the favourite theme of the late Robert Triffen for a long time. It is also in a certain sense the European choice: the creation of a common money (issued by a common central bank) preceding that of a common political power. One recalls the proposals of Keynes in 1945: the stabilization of a compromise among the partners – the United States, the Europe of the EC and Japan. But is this stabilization possible? Is the question not a bit naive, perhaps? What can be done so that this regulation in common would be enforceable if there are no sanctions on the nations that are parties to the system? The economists, by dint of their refusal to see that economic choices are practicable only if the political and social compromises that they imply are acceptable, are encouraging a utopian economism. As we shall see eventually, a bank that is European but not worldwide is not only likely to be possible but is essential if Europe is to evolve toward a genuine political confederation. I shall also say why it can only be based on the principles of an historical social compromise, analogous on this level to the historic social compromises which have established the national states of the continent.

In any case, this – option/restraint on the partners of the developed world implies tacitly the collective recompradorization or 'sharing' of the Third World nations of the South and East. Besides the fact that the partners of the developed world agree on this matter – for example, Germany can again pursue its objective (since the days of Bismarck) to Latin Americanize Eastern Europe – it is quite evident that this recompradorization implies vigorous and permanent interventions to stifle the revolts it will certainly provoke.

(3) The third proposition is the extension of the monetary compromise to include the Third Worlds of the South and East. This was the proposal of the New International Economic Order (NIEO) put forward by the Group of Seven (G7) in 1975. This is the question of creating an international currency, at the outset in parallel with those already in use (the dollar, gold and the other key instruments), managed by the international community. Creating a link between the issue of this money and economic development was explicitly the objective. As we know, the proposal was aborted in favour of a minor international money issued by the IMF under the name of the Special Drawing Right (SDR). The reason for the defeat is evident to me: the proposition assumed that the fundamental problem was solved, that is, that the centres would accept an accelerated and relatively autonomous development of the peripheries. The monetary instrument was put in the service of this objective, which was utopian since it was in contradiction with capitalism as it really exists.

An Alternative Vision: Polycentric Regionalization

The principles on which I base the propositions that follow are consonant with an alternative vision of world political organization, that of a polycentric regionalization. This option proceeds from the contention that the real problems with which nations and regions are confronted are not identical and cannot be in view of their unequal development. It sets for itself the primary objective of reducing this inequality in which the polarization produced by the world expansion of capitalism manifests itself. It recognizes a place for globalization, on condition that it conceives itself in a manner appropriate to serving the primary objective. It recognizes at the same time that the realization of a superior world development requires the realization of regional solidarities and autonomies, articulated in the world system by mechanisms and institutions that owe their existence to the heritage of unequal development. Finally, it associates at each stage the rules that govern the regulation of the economy and money with parallel propositions on the institutions of politics.

It is a matter therefore of a voluntarist project. More exactly, if one regards it as a 'utopia', it is not that it is utopian in the same sense in which regulation of the world by the market is utopian. The latter is a true utopia: if one tries to pursue its project one can only create a catastrophe. By contrast, the project that we propose, if embarked upon, will gradually ameliorate the conditions at which it is directed. Therefore, if one were to call it utopian, it is simply in the sense that the dominant political forces that are active today do not work in its direction. The implementation of this project in effect implies marked transformations in the nature of the powers and interests that are to be served, and in the futures that are to be envisioned.

The regions in question here almost define themselves. If the United States (eventually enlarged by incorporating Canada but not Mexico), China and India (by virtue of their demographic weight) and Japan (by virtue of its history) constitute by themselves regions, all the other countries of the world ought to envision their consolidation into an ensemble of great regions: Europe (East and West), the former Soviet Union, the Arab world, the African world, South-East Asia and Latin America.

The problems with which these regions and countries are confronted are too varied for one to suppose that they should all develop along the same lines. For example, there is no sense in which the rate of interest should be the same everywhere or that capital should flow freely to wherever the pecuniary return is the highest. Monetary and financial institutions must be developed along regional lines as substitutes for the IMF and the world market for monetary capital.

The Europe of the EC is going in this direction, although it is in some sense the sick man among regions, having developed a purely economistic concept of its project ('an integrated market', no more), and finds itself confronted with a great problem, which is to endow itself with corresponding political power. But while the social sorting-out of this project remains to be done, the common market, which is only a hollow shell, will engender insurmountable social (and therefore political) conflicts. The further consolidation of the European economies will require regulation by a state, perhaps confederal, capable of imposing a labour/capital compromise on the scale of the integrated market. The traditional Right will never, by its nature, understand this necessity, preoccupied as it is with exploiting the differences in the short term. Just as not long ago it was the workers' movement which imposed a social compromise on the scale of the European national states, today on the scale of Europe it is only a courageous and farsighted Left that could lead the way. Eventually there would have to be brought into being a system issuing an intra-European money to substitute for the national monies, to the extent that there is progress towards a common political construct that can give legitimacy to common financial and monetary institutions.

Can Eastern Europe be integrated into the European system? Perhaps, but only on the condition that the West Europeans do not see the peoples of the East as their 'Latin Americans'. Overcoming the unequal development of Europe will require the articulation of pan-European institutions that tolerate the different rules of the game in the different halves of the continent. A long transition is therefore necessary before the economic and political integration of Europe can reach its ultimate phase.

Russia and the other states of the former Soviet Union are in a situation of the same nature even if, by virtue of its size, Russia remains potentially a great power. The reconstruction of cooperation and integration among these countries is a necessary stage if one wishes to avoid the explosive danger of their unequal development.

The European construct, even reduced to the partners of the EC, runs the risk of again becoming bogged down in questioning its reason for being. The absence of agreement among the West Europeans on peripheralizing Eastern Europe and the former Soviet Union, which is being encouraged by the countries of the East themselves – the Czechs separate from the Slovaks because they think this puts them nearer to integration with the EC, the Croats decide to precipitate the collapse of Yugoslavia, the Baltic countries and the Croats separate themselves from the Russians for similar reasons – reveals the conflicts at the heart of the EC itself. It is almost evident then that this option will lead Germany to charge ahead on its own, forcing its partners to follow up to the point where the situation becomes unacceptable and the European project disintegrates. In this scenario the 'European central bank' – which will then be a *de facto* annex of the Bundesbank – runs the risk of becoming merely a temporary instrument in the service of a German, rather than a European, project.

The problems of the regions of the Third World are different to the degree that their underdevelopment is more marked. For these reasons: (i) these countries and regions are less thoroughly integrated into the global production system that is under construction. Except for Korea, Taiwan and Singapore, which are the only important exceptions (Hong Kong being partially integrated with China), in all the semi-industrialized countries of the Third World only limited segments of the productive system are integrated into the new global economy; (ii) they are even less integrated among themselves, practically not at all, especially when it comes to the Fourth World; (iii) they are unevenly developed, and the postwar period has accentuated this inequality, which even today separates the semi-industrialized countries from those of the Fourth World; finally, (iv) for all these reasons they are attracted by regional North–South associations which operate to the detriment of their collective autonomy.

Under these conditions the creation of regional monetary institutions is not a priority. Before this will be the order of the day it will be necessary to pass through some preliminary stages that emphasize the construction of negotiated and well-conceived productive complementarities. At this stage the common regional monetary institutions that are the most appropriate are endeavours such as accords on multilateral clearing, payments unions, etc., which permit partial escape from such constraints as the need to hold national reserves of key currencies. But it goes without saying that here as elsewhere progress on regional economic integration requires the *rapprochement* of national policies. The putting into place of the embryos of confederal organizations should not be postponed; quite the contrary. In parallel with the democratization of national systems, one can imagine that leagues of Arab peoples, of African peoples, of Latin American peoples and of South-East Asian peoples will gradually be substituted for the present-day state organizations.

The collective international negotiations that these ensembles of regional, economic, monetary and political institutions require goes without saying. At the monetary level a reconstituted IMF will find a new function in regulating the relations among the dollar, the yen, the European currencies, the rouble, and the payment arrangements among the regions of the Third World. But this reform will not assume its real significance until, in its turn, the United Nations is transformed to become a real player in international affairs instead of the enforcer of the policies of the United States and its partners in the North. In this spirit the World Bank, which has up to now been the bank of the North in its policies toward the South, will be equally reformed and become the embryo of a world capital market that assists regionally coordinated development policies negotiated collectively.

A utopian project? It is the only way, in my opinion, that can help us find a way out of the tragic impasse of the present crisis and start us on the long trail toward socialism, the only possible human response.

CHAPTER 4

The Rise of Ethnicity: A Political Response to Economic Globalization

The present epoch is surely characterized by an awakening, or re-awakening, marked by collective social identifications which are starkly different from those defined by membership of a nation-state or a social class. Regionalism, linguistic and cultural assertion, tribal or ethnic loyalties, devotion to a religious group, attachment to a local community, are some of the multiple forms this re-awakening has taken. In both East and West, or in the countries of the Third World, it would be a lengthy business to draw up a complete list of these new movements, or rather old-style movements now revived. They constitute an important aspect of the crisis of the state, and more particularly of the nation-state, however notional the nation in question may in reality be. In my opinion, this crisis of the state is the product of the growing contradiction between the transnationalization of capital (and behind it the globalization of economic life of the capitalist countries of the world generally) on the one side, and on the other the persistence of the idea that the state is the only political system that exists in our world. The question raised here, however, is: why, in circumstances where capital is becoming increasingly internationalized, are the peoples of the world not responding to this by internationalizing themselves, that is, by affirming their class allegiance across national boundaries? Why, instead of asserting itself, is class consciousness giving way to self-identification by 'race', 'ethnic group' or religion?

The media, with their usual ideological crassness, generally respond that it is so because 'people are like that'. In the depths of the soul, there is a latent racial, ethnic or religious consciousness which is bursting forth, and which is something that the bourgeois, democratic or secular ideologies, be they socialist or Marxist, have always underestimated.

This is an unsatisfactory type of response. I propose, therefore, to analyse this phenomenon from the standpoint of the movement of capital accumulation, which governs all contemporary systems, both local and global, and in relation to the successive and contrasting phases of this movement, its periods of success and its times of crisis. I shall confine myself strictly to the strategies of the social actors – that is, of capital and the dominant classes on the one hand, and of the various peoples and popular classes on the other; to the characteristics of these successive movements to the challenge they represent; and to the various actors' perceptions of them. Within this framework I further propose an analysis of the various social realities, other than social classes defined by their modes of production, which make up the fabric of society (for example, the nation and the ideology of the nation, ethnicity and the ethnic ideology) and with which class is situated within the movement of history. From there, I propose to gauge the directions in which history is guiding the evolution of both the local and the global systems.

The Postwar Cycle (1945-90) and the New Globalization

As it emerged from the Second World War, capitalism, which had really become the world economic system, retained two characteristics inherited from its historical evolution:

(1) The historically constructed bourgeois nation-states (which together constituted the centres of the world system). They represented the political and social framework for the management of national capitalist economies (national systems of production controlled and governed largely by national capital), each in aggressive competition with the others.

(2) An almost absolute contrast between the industrialization of the centres and the absence of industry in the peripheries, resulting from these centres' successive industrialization during the course of the nineteenth century.

During the postwar cycle, however, these two characteristics disappeared steadily.

The countries on the periphery in Asia and Africa regained their independence and entered the age of industrialization, albeit in an unequal fashion, to the point where their apparent homogeneity, a product of a common previous absence of any unindustrialized industry, gave way to growing differentiation between a semi-industrialized Third World and an unindustrialized Fourth World. The interpenetration of capital was so widespread that the national productive systems were dismantled and re-established as segments of a globalized productive system.

The postwar cycle can today be regarded, therefore, as a period of transition from the old system to the new. This raises the question of how to identify this new system and its essential characteristics and contradictions and how these are controlled – identifying, in short, the moving forces behind its development.

Answering these questions must necessarily combine an analysis of the laws governing the accumulation of capital with many of the various ideological and political responses to the challenges posed by the logic of capitalism's expansion. As a result, the future is always uncertain, because the evolution of a truly existing capitalism is in its turn constrained by the need for political compromise between various social interests. The interpenetration of capital was so widespread that national productive systems disintegrated and re-established as segments of a globalized productive system. I shall here recall briefly the answers which I have proposed during the course of the last few years, notably in *The Empire of Chaos* (1993):

(1)   The industrialization of the Third World will not put an end to the polarization inherent in existing world capitalism, but will move the mechanisms and forms to other planes, governed by financial, technological, cultural and military monopolies from which the centre might benefit. It will not reproduce the same social evolution as it did in the developed West, where Fordism appeared once society had been transformed over a long period by heavy mechanical industry, sustained by a continuous agricultural revolution; where emigration to the Americas offered a way out of the pressures created by Europe's demographic explosion; and where colonial conquest enabled the acquisition of cheap raw materials. Fordism came to comfort the historic capital/labour compromise, eased by the reduction of the labour reserve in the centres.

The industrializing Third World in contrast had none of these favourable conditions by which capitalism could avoid taking on primitive forms. My argument here is that the relationship between the active workforce and the labour reserve exploited by capital, which developed in the history of the centres, cannot reproduce itself in the periphery. The criterion used here to define the boundaries between the active workforce and the reserve labour force must be, in conformity with the logic of capitalist globalization, employment in parts of the more-or-less competitive worldwide productive systems. Using this criterion one could say that in the centres the great majority of labour participates effectively in the active workforce, because the historical make-up of central capitalisms, has, slowly and progressively, developed favourable conditions which cannot be reproduced outside this situation. In the industrialized peripheries of Latin America, of East Asia (both communist and capitalist) and the countries of the former Soviet Union, the various sectors of the productive system are already, or could become, competitive in the given sense of the word. Here an active labour force exists and is able to follow its course. But however far ahead one may look, it could never absorb the reserve of the rural and informal economies. This is because competitiveness today requires production techniques which make such an absorption impossible, and because the safety-valve of emigration does not exist.

In the non-industrialized and non-competitive peripheries of Africa and the Arab world, the situation is even more extreme: here the active workforce is practically non-existent, with almost the entire nation constituting a labour reserve on a world scale.

In the industrialized Third World the coexistence of a growing active workforce and a huge labour reserve causes intense and potentially revolutionary social conflict. This situation, which has become characteristic of modern peripheral capitalism, gives rise to favourable political and ideological conditions for the construction of national and popular alliances around the working class: of peasants overexploited by the financial burden which expansion has placed on them and the mass of the marginalized poor who make up the reserve labour force. In the Fourth World, excluded from industrialization at this stage, the social system takes on an extreme appearance: the great majority of the people are the reserve force which brings together both the marginalized poor and the peasant masses excluded from any agricultural revolution. Confronted by these popular classes the minorities in power cannot assert any historical legitimacy whatsoever.

(2) In the developed West, the conflict between the logic of the interpenetration of capital eroding the efficacy of the nation-state and the permanence of political and ideological systems based on national realities will before long prohibit any satisfactory response to the crisis. Neither the hegemony of the United States, called upon to function solely on the military plane, nor the

building of a unified Europe such as is presently conceived (a 'supermarket' unaccompanied by any progressive social policy, which would call for a real federal policy) can cope with the challenges. In any case, the European project operates in a conjunction marked by the aggravation of inter-European inequalities (German domination), rather than harnessing regions of the South and East to each of the three centres which make up the developed North.

(3) The collapse of the Soviet system has served to enlarge the field of expansion of peripheral capitalism. No conditions exist there for the crystallization of Western-style social-democratic responses.

Each of the two successive phases of globalized accumulation has provided a particular setting for political and social struggles.

I have elsewhere defined the postwar cycle as a long period of progress standing on three pillars partly conflicting but also complementary (see Chapter 3, this volume, p. 46). This three-pillar system provided the basis for an economic growth which was generally strong in each of its three regional components. It reinforced the power of the centripetal forces, guaranteeing cohesion among the different social actors, even if they were in conflict, by defining the boundaries of these conflicts.

In the developed West, it was the period of the establishment of the European Economic Community (EEC, now referred to as the European Community, or EC), which easily broadened the horizon of national expansion of its members: catching up with the United States. Social struggles remained strictly economic (for a share in the fruits of growth) and were played out on the field of national social compromise. In the Third World the national liberation movements, which brought people together on a national or pseudonational (multi-ethnic) basis in their struggle for independence, established the new state – most often autocratic (on the model of the single party) – and assured the rise of modernization. This took various forms, according to the nature of the social forces which made up the national movement: from a subordinate neocolonial capitalism to a so-called socialist project (reformist radical nationalism in fact), by way of vigorous national capitalist projects (South Korea, for example). But everywhere the centripetal forces dominated the scene and expressed themselves, in the power-base and the ruling classes through the project of nation-building. The nascent new bourgeoisie was united. It was the same in the so-called socialist countries of the East, where growth consolidated the dominant class and even sometimes ensured, at least partially, the rallying of the popular classes to the nation-building project.

The deployment of the various projects, and even their success, was due to ideological illusions, which nevertheless worked strongly on popular opinion. In the West it was believed that continuous growth was permanent; in the Third World it was believed that building the nation would eventually resolve the problems of underdevelopment; in the East people believed in 'socialism'.

The reversal of circumstances which put an end to this phase of expansion resulted from the demolition of the postwar tripolar system. Every region of the globe was plunged into a profound and lasting structural crisis, with no indication of any light at the end of the tunnel, either in the West, the East, or the South. The dominant discourse of even the strongest powers became that of crisis management rather than that of solutions. In the West, for example, there is no longer any talk of ending unemployment, but rather of 'living with the problem'. One speaks of an economy travelling at 'two speeds'.

Such periods of systemic structural crisis are always those when the centrifugal forces are at the fore. The disarray which is a product of stagnation and a regression of social and economic conditions (and at the same time of a superstructure characterized by the disappearance of illusion, for which the peoples were unprepared) strengthens these centrifugal forces.

In the always fragile peripheries these centrifugal forces have broken the unity of the ruling classes, and reduced them to desperate straits. Suddenly they appear to have lost all the legitimacy upon which their power rested. Our hypothesis is that the political crises are founded on this breakdown, on this disintegration of the state, and the accompanying rise of ethnic movements and religious fundamentalism. It then remains for us to analyse how these reversals of ideological conviction and of political behaviour function, how they find or create the forces necessary to sustain their project. It remains to be seen what strategies imperialism will deploy to confront them or manipulate them to advantage.

Even in the developed centres, where the effects of the crisis of capital are less dramatic, the centrifugal forces seem, nevertheless, to have found a hitherto unknown space in which to operate. It is sometimes said that there is an ideological crisis of the nation-state. More simply, for the politicians, the crisis is intensifying already-existing contradictions at the heart of various projects, such as that of the EC, which appeared previously to be forging ahead.

The Disintegration of the State and the New Ethnic Ideologies in the Third World

In the peripheral regions of the Third World, particularly those which make up the Fourth World, the crisis has not only eroded the surplus but has sometimes wiped it out completely, thus not even ensuring the simple reproduction of the system. With the breakup of the power base and of the ruling class, the disintegration of the country takes on an extreme form as, for example, in Somalia.

In Africa the dissolution of national unity sometimes seems to have given way to ethnicity as a basis for the legitimate renewal of competing forces. But Africa is not the only terrain where these centrifugal forces are deployed. In India, in Afghanistan, in Eastern Europe, in the former Soviet Union and the former Yugoslavia, even in Western Europe, in Spain, for example, and possibly even in Italy, national unity has been put in question.

It is always the case that the apparent success of such unfolding ethnic movements poses a problem. Do those aspiring to power find their 'ethnic groups' already in place, occupying the field and naturally disposed to follow them? This view of the problem is, in my opinion, too simplistic. I will be content with recalling the conclusions at which I have arrived, and which the reader will find elaborated in *Maldevelopment* (pp. 147–55).

(1) An ethnic group constitutes no more than a 'race' or any other 'non-reality' invented to serve the cause of the social organization of the precapitalist world.

The existence of a variety of peoples was recognized in the map of Africa, and of other regions of the world, in the precapitalist epoch. 'Peoples' is a general term and one which does not imply any *a priori* qualification. These peoples were organized in spaces which did not necessarily coincide with matrimonial exchanges but were rather defined by exchanges over a wider distance, by the eventual centralization of the surplus, by political organization and eventually the centralized state, by the mythologies of ancestry and of origin, by religious beliefs and common languages. This cartography of defined spaces could be continued almost indefinitely.

Where does the ethnic group belong in this multiform reality? Everywhere and nowhere. At various stages in these systems, there is a sense of community which doesn't necessarily develop into a sense of ethnic belonging. There is the village community and that of the villages surrounded by the same elementary dependent unity and/or intricate matrimonial relations; there are the wider spaces, often vaguely religious, for example, the Christian in medieval Europe. Language itself does not of necessity give rise to a sense of community. In our times, when the state/scholarly system is largely unified and has imposed a single language, one tends to forget that ancient peoples are often polyglot (look at Africa), that they use one language or another, variant or idiom, according to circumstance, without, in the language of the linguistic chauvinists, making a problem of this multiple identity.

(2) Precapitalist society is not necessarily homogeneous. There are always zones of a denser crystallization of population, development of the productive forces, and political and cultural-religious forces; and intermediate zones, dependent more or less on the former, which have escaped the homogenization imposed by the development of the larger states. But there are no minorities in the modern sense of the term. Plurality is the norm. It is only the standardizing practices of the capitalist market, generally education in a so-called national language and the ideology of the nation which accompanies this, which, in the modern age, have transformed certain groups into new minorities. (See my *The Strategic Stakes in the Mediterranean*, pp. 97–8, for a development of this theme in relation to the Arab world.)

(3) In the case of the Arab world, I have spoken of a quasi-nation superimposing itself upon a regional community, based on the centralization and circulation of a surplus guaranteed by the dominant class of warrior-traders. This class was strongly unified in the great era (it spread from Tangier to Baghdad without this causing any problem) by way of, among other means, a written language and religion. It was still a quasi-nation because the productive forces did not to any large extent integrate the peasant masses, particularly those which were geographically isolated, particularly during the periods of the decline of long-distance trade. But the unity of this ruling class is strong, hence our qualification. Nonetheless, there is no 'Arab ethnic group'; not even the surviving enclaves have an ethnic consciousness (for example the Berbers do not consider themselves to be 'a people').

(4) The case of West Africa presents the greatest similarities with that of North Africa. In this respect I propose: (i) that the great states of West Africa (Ghana, Mali, Songhai) were founded on control of the southern reaches of Saharan trade, as those of the north were based on control of its northern reaches; (ii) that the ruling class of these states, far from being assimilable into one dominant ethnicity, was formed on the basis of some warring clans, largely open to assimilation (there are therefore people who are Malinke or Songhai by profession, just as there were those who were Turks by profession during the Ottoman Empire); (iii) that the space of these dominations, with fluctuating borders, remained strongly heterogeneous, even irregular, notably from the point of view of what is today called 'ethnicity'.

(5) The practices of colonial domination have played a determining role in the creation of ethnic realities. In order to gain control of vast areas, often in disarray following the decline of the slave trade, the colonizers had to reorganize, and for this purpose needed local intermediaries. In the absence of states, or of a dependent or feudal class, the colonizers invented the 'chief' and rigged him out with powers he had never previously had. But what exactly was he to be 'chief' of? It was then that the colonial administrators and the military, poor amateur anthropologists that they were, invented 'tribes'.

(6) It is impossible to remake history. And so, evolutionary product of history or not, if the tribe exists, then it has to be recognized. But does ethnicity really exist, and if so, where?

In certain cases, it seems obvious that an ethnic reality is false, that it is, rather, an attribute of the current political situation. On closer examination, however, it can be seen that in the majority of cases this reality is manipulated by clans competing for power within the ruling class. But has ethnicity been truly internalized by the masses? This remains to be proved. In Katanga, for example (the Shaba of today), one could hardly speak of ethnicity, but rather of provincialism, itself multi-ethnic. This provincialism was nothing more than a reflection of the backwardness of the local petit bourgeoisie of this region dominated by the great mining capital, confronted by the petit bourgeoisie of Kinshasa, which in the early 1960s was radical nationalist. Here again, imperialism took advantage of the contradiction in order to prolong its control over Katanga, which was threatened by rising support for Lumumba. But once colonial power rested in Kinshasa, imperialism shifted the gun to the other shoulder. (This provincialism, which soon became known in the Western media as 'tribalism', was of no concern to the great mass of the people: the first provincial workers' organizations laid no claim to any ethnic basis whatsoever.)

Though in a number of African countries the spectre of ethnicity and ethnicism is always ready to raise its head each time the local ruling class starts to disintegrate, this is not the case in general. A stable neocolonial power is based on a ruling class that is more or less unified at the level of the state, and is largely multi-ethnic. In the main a comprador class, its fate is tied up with the state through which it is able to exercise power. Doubtless, its constituent members may look to their region of origin for a clientele since they are not allowed to make use of the normal political means to maintain power. They are liable, consequently, to appeal to 'ethnic' solidarities. This type of manipulation has, however, a limited effect, which is aggravated only in the case of global instability when imperialism itself seems to have decided to change course.

(7) Ethnicity is not the only centrifugal movement produced by the crisis of accumulation, nor the only recourse of certain segments of a shattered ruling class trying to re-establish some legitimate basis for its power. Manipulation of democracy is another means of trying to get out of the impasse. Instead of a unanimous rallying around a single party in the name of development, there instead occours a proliferation of groups, all emerging from the same class, all trying to appear different beneath the mantle of multi-partyism. Calling for freedom, wary of questioning the real forces behind the crisis, all in agreement with economic liberalization and privatization, many turn to ethnicity. In other historical conjunctions religious fundamentalism fulfils the same role. (For further reading on this point see, for example, *Eurocentrism*.)

Globalization and the Crisis of Nationhood

Here I will summarize the conclusions put forward in *Maldevelopment* (pp. 127–47): see my remarks on p. 62 above.

1. The nation-state is an historical product, one which is localized in time and space. Nineteenth-century Europe remains central to our modern history. It was during the course of these decades that the foundations of the national bourgeois state, the framework of our contemporary world, were laid, through all manner of decisive struggles.

Two contradictory collections of theories were produced within this framework: Marxism and the theory of class struggles on the one hand; nationalism and the theory of the integration of classes in a bourgeois democratic nation-state on the other. Both took account of many aspects of the immediate reality, which was marked by social struggles which even became revolutionary, and by struggles between nation-states which went on to become wars. Both established instruments capable of inspiring the actions of the protagonists which are the subjects of history and think of themselves as such.

The effectiveness of political strategies, however, arises from a specific conjuncture defined by a coincidence, limited in time and space, between: (i) the state and that other social reality, the nation; (ii) the dominant position of the bourgeois nation-states, situated within the world capitalist system, their central characteristic; and (iii) a certain level of globalization of the autocentric central economic units, interdependent but with a high degree of autonomy.

One may then begin to understand why this conjuncture is able to give effectiveness to policies inspired by these theories. However much in conflict relations between the classes may be, they are regulated in and by the nation-state. In this sense there exists an average price for the national workforce, determined by history and by the interrelationship of the classes, a national system reflecting decisive social relations. The law of value has a national dimension. Nations and classes — workers, bourgeoisie, peasants — are effective subjects of history.

What is the role in the conjuncture of this 'national' reality that we have not yet determined? Ideology will subsequently give it an autonomous dimension, attributing a pre-existence to the state, a stance which seems to us debatable. Nevertheless, in this case the nation is surely a product of capitalism, as Marxism and conventional sociology have also recognized.

2. The strength of the earlier mode of the nation has inspired those which came later. Since there already existed an English nation and a French nation, the German and Italian nations took them as models in creating their own states. The political intelligence of the creators lay in knowing how to forge alliances and social compromises capable of mobilizing the various forces in support.

3. In the European nation-states the linguistic dimension gained exceptional strength which possibly even constituted the essence of the nation as a new social achievement. Education and modern democracy have made of the national language an instrument which ends by defining the nation itself, its boundaries, its mass culture.

4. On closer examination, however, it seems that this powerful coincidence of the nineteenth century was in fact very limited in space.

The European semi-peripheries – the Austro-Hungarian and the Russian empires – evolved in the sense of a central evolution, and not without difficulty. The beginning of a unified capitalist market constituted a challenge to the old dynastic state. This challenge would be met by an unhesitating renovation/modernization which had recourse to great means: education, and constitutional and social reform. But here, the imported nationalist ideology was a handicap rather than a driving force. It finished by destroying the Austro-Hungarian Empire. And if the Russian Empire survived until 1990 – thanks to the Bolshevik Revolution – it was doubtless due in great part to the fact that the Russian nation predominated. Today the crisis in Eastern Europe once more puts in doubt the future of the countries that belong to it: will they be absorbed by the movement of developed European capitalism, or in their turn be thrust onto the periphery, in other words, 'Latin Americanized'?

Therein lies one of the displacements which constitute the hypothesis of this reflection. For it is not said that the Czech, Slovak, Polish, Hungarian, Slovenian, Croatian, and German bourgeoisies – each had a need for 'their' state and 'their' markets. It is never said that they could have made up the segments of a single bourgeoisie based on a single integrated market. It is not obvious that the peasant masses would prefer to be exploited by their national bourgeoisie. The conflict is characteristically polarized around language, largely by a projection of the new role language is playing in developed Western Europe. The complicated game of real and potential social conflict leads the political forces – social-democratic parties of the Second International, peasant parties, new bourgeois parties – to theorize, justify and propose endless strategies which finally fall back on the myth of the idealized nation-state unified by language.

In all cases the result has been mediocre. After 1920 the inheriting states confirmed the local bourgeois hegemonies as incompetent, and quickly fell into the lap either of Berlin or of Paris. The potential for capitalist development was wasted, economic stagnation became marked. After the Second World War the system inspired and imposed by the Soviet model began a new history. Not all in this new history was negative, nor can one say that the fate of the peoples of the region would have been any better otherwise or that they would have then avoided their peripheralization. But it is also not certain that they are equipped to avoid this today.

5. The ideology of the nation-state is so strong that when, after the Second World War, all countries of the world achieved independence, they all constituted a system of nation-states, precisely at that very moment when the nation-state entered a crisis which now seems endless, even in its centres of origin.

6. The globalization of the capitalist system during the period 1945–70 attained, in effect, a stage which has given it characteristics which are qualitatively new.

Until the middle of our century globalization operated in a market which was international rather than global, and which gave the law of value a national content, within the framework of constraints imposed in international competition by the embryo of a global law of capitalist value. At this stage, the social classes were still essentially national classes, defined by social relations established within the limits of the state. There was, therefore, a conjunction between class struggle and the political game, which was regulated precisely within the framework of these states.

After the Second World War, the break-up of national systems of production and their recomposition as elements of a globalized system began. In *The Empire of Chaos* (Chapters 1 and 3) I propose a critical examination of the new contradictions created by this evolution, and I place emphasis on the utopianism of administering the system by means of unilateral submission to the so-called regulation of the market. Since there is no planetary state, and the United States, which had partially adopted this function is itself in crisis, since the global institutions are still embryonic, and the political games (like elections) still establish themselves on the basis of the state system, any coincidence between the conflicts and compromises of class on the one hand, and politics on the other, has disappeared.

Europe itself is threatened by this economistic utopianism. The establishment of the Common Market, which has (almost) become the single market, has been done without any parallel development of political institutions for its administration (see Chapter 6 in this book for an elaboration of this argument). The project has progressed largely because of the success of the previous phase, so that the establishment of political means for its definitive anchorage has always been repulsed.

And yet suddenly, with the re-establishment of a unified Germany, the balance of forces within Europe itself has been upset. Is it not possible that Germany will henceforth pursue its own objectives – the Latin-Americanization of Eastern Europe for its own profit – without too much thought for its partners? (Or only if they agree to play a secondary role in this new German Europe?) The indications are that this is so. Nevertheless, in the longer term it has not been said that the awakening of the old European nations will not throw the present options of this continent into question, in the West as well as the East .

The utopia of the market also lies at the heart of the degradation of the democratic policies of the West itself. The unilateral submission to this constraint, operating by means of the bias of international competition, has brought about political inefficiency and created a state of unease. The history of the United States, once more in advance of that of Europe, has shown how this vacuum can be filled by a combination of permanent elements (perhaps racism, or religious and social deviations, fulfil a useful function in this instability?) and of conglomerates of differing interests (for example, professional and local lobbies). And aren't there signs of similar phenomena appearing in Europe?

7. In general, capitalist expansion has inverse effects upon the centres and the peripheries of the system; in the first it integrates society, on which the nation is based, and in the second it destroys society, eventually destroying the nation itself, or annihilating its potentialities. This asymmetry about the economic basis of the system is essential. It reflects the qualitatively different position of the local bourgeoisies at the local and global levels.

In the societies which it has pushed to the periphery the expansion of capital has run up against diverse and unequally developed forms of organization.

Was China also on the point of inventing capitalism? Would capitalism too, on the basis of a substratum already present, have reinforced the Chinese nation? Has this maturity enabled China to avoid the worst: disintegration? Or is it the seed of Confucius and simply the size of the continent which has made it hesitate to conquer? India aroused no fear, neither in Duplessis nor the East India Company. But there the nation-state, despite its decadence, still with hindsight appears as a subject for history. It made up the framework – national is the only term which imposes itself – within which the historical subjects which make up the various classes confronted each other under the successive hegemonies of the aristocracy and the bureaucracy (then bourgeois). Its transformation was finally ruled by a peasant revolution directed by the Communist Party.

Ramkrishna Mukerjee (1976) has demonstrated the reality of India's early capitalist development. Indian unity is not, as one is wont to say too quickly, the product of British colonialism. Hinduism certainly formed a real common denominator; but it also operates in a family of a dozen nations. The unification of the capitalist market has not yet been brought about even by the wish of the bourgeoisies of these different countries to break up the new state for their own profit, as was the case in Central and Eastern Europe. Is it because the ideology of the nation-state had not penetrated here, in this part of the world less clouded by the Western European model than Austro-Hungary or the Balkans?

The Ottoman and the Egyptian states likewise provide food for thought. The maturation of capitalist relations is evident in the Balkans, in Egypt and in Syria. The state which superimpose itself on the various peoples which comprise it – Arab and Turkish Muslims, Greek Christians, Slavs and Armenians – was not a natural obstacle to this maturation. Its incapacity to resist the positioning regulated by foreign capital eventually ended by making it lose its legitimacy. But there too, just as in Central Europe, the proof will be found in the history of the inheriting states that offered hardly any more resistance. Nevertheless the echo of the ideology of the nation-state on the European model had a great effect on the 'young Turks' who, taking the initiative and creating an albeit artificial idea of a Turkish perspective, completed what the Kemalist revolution had started. As in Central Europe, this choice would finish by making Turkey the 'lumpen nation' of a Europe which rejected it. In a predictable echo, the liberal Egyptian bourgeoisie rallied to this thesis during the period between the two world wars. This option, then abandoned by a return to an Arab Egypt, finds an objective basis in the 'double layer' of the Arab nation.

In the Americas, too, in an historical substratum albeit very different, the state operates likewise as an active subject, forging the nation, or with the intention of doing so, with more or less success. In the United States the foundation was provided by the construction of an autocentric base from New England, which extended to the whole country after the question of the South was settled. But the nation did not succeed in building itself in Latin America, despite its countries' early independence. The peripheralization of the basis of the economy kept it beyond the reach of the formal state. This anyway consisted of a state made up of Creoles, who kept the Indian communities marginalized. We can only really speak of a nation-state in Mexico where, with the revolution of the twentieth century, the Hispanization of the Indian communities made decisive progress. In all cases in Latin America, in this area as in others, the European model remained the sole point of reference and, with it, the undisputed ideology of the nation-state.

Will the global crisis of accumulation of our age call into question the national unity of the states of the Third World?

In India, for example, the compradorization of the bourgeoisie – which had been able to pass through various stages of national (but not popular) development – has placed the unity of the state at risk. It has reinforced regional irredentisms, manipulated by cliques whose aim is to control local politics, and thrown into question the pan-Indian alliance of the ruling classes (large landowners of the North, the techno-bureaucracy, industrial capitalists, merchant capitalists, kulaks).

Will not Mexico's association with the United States and Canada in a common market run the risk of splitting the country into a 'Texan' and a 'Guatemalan' Mexico, thus reproducing the break which enabled the United States in the 19th century to annex half of Mexico as it then was. And in the Arab and Islamic world, doesn't religious fundamentalism, whose rise has occurred in response to compradorization, threaten to annihilate a whole century of efforts towards modernization and 'national' construction?

In contrast to these negative developments, one may observe that the types of development in East Asia are assuming particular and strongly distinguishing characteristics. While elsewhere in the Third World the expansion of the internal market was based on a relative increase of the income of the middle classes to the detriment of the popular masses, in East Asia, exceptionally, all salaries (including those of the middle strata) have been kept to a minimum, allowing for huge savings, generally public, while the peasant income has been sensibly raised. In the Chinese states of Taiwan, Hong Kong and Singapore, a close collaboration has been established between the foreign Chinese bourgeoisie, spreading across the whole of the Western Pacific and South-East Asia. At a demographic level Confucian Asia has attained a modest level of growth which translates into a wider social command and a wider penetration of the ideal of personal and familial enrichment. Finally, the efforts made in the area of technical education have been much more systematic and efficient. Working on the basis of a strong national reality, these developments are forging the emergence of a hegemonic national bourgeoisie, legitimized by a fairly broad social consensus, much closer than elsewhere.

Nevertheless, the crisis reveals the vulnerability of strategies based on a deliberate insertion into the international division of labour. Better able than Latin America or the Arab world to manage the eventual readjustments imposed by the external crisis, Confucian Asia can also, if necessary, be self-reliant. An intensification of the relations of these countries with China and Japan could be profitable to all the partners and modify significantly the global balance of forces.

8. In the countries of ex-'socialist' Eastern Europe, a page of history has been turned. From between 40 to 70 years, according to the particular situation, the region's constituent countries attempted to overcome the legacy of their former peripheralization. The local bourgeoisie had failed to achieve the building of a modern self-reliant economy, taking part both in the world system and the parallel one of the nation. Would the new so-called socialist powers be able to ? I will not here return to the critical evaluation of these experiences, and to the reasons which led me to the conclusion that, far from building socialism, these powers were constructing a bourgeoisie, and were, therefore, building capitalism, albeit within a framework of a statist option delinked from the pressures of the world system. I have concluded that the collapse of these systems was not the product of a democratic revolution, nor a counter-revolution, but only the final phase of their natural development.

It is true that the economic, ideological and political crises of this collapse have also brought down the ruling class in all these countries. Here once more we find the ethnic or national factor at work. In the multinational countries (USSR, Yugoslavia and to a lesser degree Czechoslovakia) the different parts of the ruling classes seek to find their support on the basis of ethnicity. In the others they try to mobilize national chauvinism, thence exacerbating potential conflicts with the various national minorities (for example, Hungarians in Romania). As one will see, the proposed comparison between the former Yugoslavia (a true federation whose functioning was marked by inequalities of development in favour of the less deprived states) and the former USSR (a state which was centralized in the extreme, but which organized a redistribution in favour of the most backward areas) situates the differences not only in matters concerning the immediate present but also perhaps the future. Elsewhere, the 'national question' hinges on the 'democratic question', no less manipulated by the ruling classes, and taking various forms from one country to another. Whatever the case, this combination of mediocre strategies and tactics does nothing to improve the country's chances of 'doing better' – in terms of economic development – than the statist, autocratic regimes of the so-called socialist era. On the contrary, the weakening of the entire region, Russia included, opens the way for a renewal of German expansionism.

Can China, also on the path to capitalist development, succeed in managing this passage less badly, safeguarding its national unity?

9. History leads us, by way of this overview, to question the ideology of the nation, whether in its bourgeois version (the nation is a pre-existing reality; the ideal nation – the nation-state – is built on this foundation and reveals its potential) or in its common Marxist version (capitalism has created nations and has generalized the form of the nation-state the world over). True history rather suggests that the state is the active subject which sometimes creates the nation, sometimes regenerates it, but often fails to do so. True history also suggests the importance of the ideology of the nation-state, which is not always a progressive active agent of capitalist development but a deviant which deflects direction in a negative sense or even slows down the pace of development. In the successful cases, the nation becomes an active historical subject, a framework for conflict and compromise between its citizens, who constitute the social classes of capitalism or have emerged from them. Elsewhere, whether the economic base remains, or becomes, peripheral, the state grows weak or disappears; and whether the potential national crystallizations disintegrate or fail to do so, groups and social classes, different types of communities and the state meet in a game of conflicts which does not permit the future of the people in question to be in control.

The Current Management of the Crisis and its Alternatives

The management of the political and social systems – whether local (national) or on a global scale – by the single virtue of the market – is a utopia. It is almost amusing to observe that at the very moment that 'the end of ideologies' is proclaimed, the dominant system is attempting to impose a pure ideology, expressed in the most extreme primitive form!

This is because the dominant forces in a time of lasting structural crisis like ours are not looking for a way out at all, but only for a means of managing the crisis. Discourse proposing long-term solutions in the interest of all – such as the Brandt Report, for example – which sets off from the principle that 'we are all in the same boat', is naïve because it does not correspond to the way capitalism functions today. In reality the dominant forces generally give priority to the tactic of crisis management. In pursuing this they lay the greatest possible weight of the crisis on the shoulders of the weakest partners – the peripheries of the South and the East – with a view to alleviating the consequences of the crisis in the developed centres and ensuring that they do not in their turn become dramatic. This has worked against finding a solution. The new language of the dominant ideological apparatuses bears witness to these short-term preoccupations. Nowadays one hears of 'governance', meaning to say the 'governability' of a situation which is difficult to manage because it is in itself naturally explosive.

A function of this way of thinking is the disintegration of the peripheral states. These states are the fag-end of the world system, vulnerable in the extreme, open to world market forces and without the means to control them, so that they bear the maximum burden of the global crisis. This disastrous policy is interwoven with contradictions which are difficult to resolve. Permanent disorder manifests itself in regression and violence, and then the theory of (military) 'low-intensity conflict' management comes to the aid of the dominant powers as a means of managing these contradictions.

The methods employed are blatant manipulations: manipulations of ethnicity (or of religious fundamentalism), and of democracy, by means of selective interventions, according to the circumstances. This system would seem to rest on the basis of 'one law for the rich and another for the poor': here one intervenes on behalf of the people, there one maintains silence; here one imposes 'free' elections, there one defends a brutal dictatorship. The powers hope to get their way by domesticating the media by legitimizing interventions or maintaining a total silence when faced with more embarrassing situations. Political naïvety is also mobilized to this end: the 'humanitarian organizations', for example, allow themselves to be made use of by the powers, just as in the past the missionaries – often armed with the best of subjective intentions – accompanied colonial conquest. Once again reality has shown that the interventions of the developed West in the affairs of the Third World, whatever the motives invoked, are always negative.

The dominant tactical preoccupation does not rule out the fact that the powers which are better placed in the world chess-board are, at the same time, pursuing their own strategic objectives. Two of these objectives are clearly apparent in the cases of Eastern Europe and of Ethiopia. The first demonstrates the strategic plan of German expansionism, the second that of American hegemony. The two plans converge, at least partially. They also marginalize the other powers, France and the rest of Europe, which are forced to align themselves.

The German objective – the Latin Americanization of Eastern Europe, thus affirming German pre-eminence over the rest of Europe – coincides with that of the United States, which is to weaken Russia as much as possible in order to return to the situation of 1945, when the

United States had the monopoly of weapons of mass destruction and were thus able to impose world hegemony. Bonn has already won important points: the destruction of Yugoslavia and the compradorization of Slovenia/Croatia, Bohemia-Moravia returned to the status of protectorate, the Baltic states and the Ukraine separated from the Russians. In this arena the so-called information media have been completely mobilized, to the point of becoming worthy of the name 'media of disinformation'. Two laws again, 'one for the rich and another for the poor': the Russians, settled in the Baltic states for as long as the English in Ireland, and in greater numbers, may become deprived of the right to vote. This does not disqualify the Baltic 'democracies', whilst the Irish who find it abnormal to be under the yoke of the English remain 'terrorists'. Following on the break-up of the USSR, isn't the dismemberment of Russia, reducing it to Muscovy, a strategic objective?

The United States' objective is, whatever one may say, the maintenance of the advantages it derives from its global hegemony. Certainly this is threatened by the erosion of its competitiveness in the world economy and by the exorbitant cost of the interventions it makes to maintain this position. Confronted by increasing numbers of so-called 'enemies' now that the discipline of bipolarity has ceased to exist, the number of such interventions has necessarily grown. But wasn't the theory of low-intensity conflict-management developed precisely to respond to this situation? If necessary the weakening of these potential enemies by the disintegration of states and the draining of their forces in neverending internal conflicts can serve to put off the necessity for intervention. Geostrategy, the constant search for bases which allow for rapid intervention, and the strategy of (military) control of the world's most important natural resources, as illustrated by the Gulf War (used as a means of pressurizing its allies) – its European and Japanese competitors – are indispensable means which the United States is not likely to renounce, at least for the present. For Washington knows well that if political hegemony is lost, it would be impossible for the United States to maintain its privileged economic status, notably the use of the dollar as an international currency (by this means forcing the rest of the world to finance its deficit). Those who argue that the United States wouldn't have the necessary financial means to impose its hegemony because internal social pressures have forced it to reduce its expenditure on external interventions, forget that for it hegemony is also the best way of keeping the flux of resources in its favour.

The medium powers do not have any strategy of their own. The old colonial powers (France in Africa, for example) are trying to preserve their corrupt clienteles but do not have the means to maintain them.

The alternative solution would be to accept authentic popular changes, which are the only forces capable of putting an end to the yawning financial chasm which the neocolonial systems have become. The tenacious colonial prejudices the West and the short-term vision of the Left, incapable of imagining North–South relations outside the framework of the imperialist tradition, straight away eliminate this choice. In these conditions, everywhere in Europe the middle powers are rallying behind German hegemony, and in the Third World they contribute to the American strategy, as we have seen in the Gulf War and as we are seeing now in Ethiopia, Somalia and Angola.

There are no situations which are insurmountable, and alternative choices always exist. Capitalist globalization such as is being offered at this time of crisis, as a means of managing it, is not in itself a way of resolving the crisis. Conversely, neither does 'rejection' of globalization constitute an adequate response. 'Rejections', apparent only by the ways in which they are expressed – the turning back to ethnicity, and religious fundamentalisim – become integrated into this brutal globalization and are made use of by it. Delinking, such as I have defined it, is not to be found in these illusory and negative rejections but on the contrary by an active insertion capable of modifying the conditions of globalization.

Globalization is, for me, not a fact of modern history to be erased by an autarkic and culturalist response, but a positive fact, a progress in history. I herewith partake of the ideologies thought common to both socialist and bourgeois. But history has no end and globalization is far from being realized. Here the bourgeois and the socialist part ways. The first wishes to fix evolution, more or less submitting it to the perspective of the unilateral action of capital. Socialism on the other hand permits one to see why this capitalist globalization remains truncated, generating, reproducing and deepening global polarization step by step. The historical limit of capitalism is found exactly here: the polarized world that it creates is and will be more and more inhuman and explosive. Challenged by this enormity, socialism has a duty to propose an alternative vision of globalization, the means of achieving it in the true sense of the word and giving it a human and truly universalist character. This is, in my opinion, the challenge.

How to go forward? By means of a strategy which aims directly to transform the world system? By strategies aimed at transforming the national and regional sub-systems? How eventually to combine the two?

Neoliberal discourse cannot respond to this real challenge of globalization unless, according to its principles, it anticipates the simultaneous opening up of all frontiers, to commerce, to capital and to the migration of workers. But this discourse remains truncated, suggesting the opening of frontiers to capital but their closure to human beings. The proposed formula can therefore only serve to aggravate global polarization.

This formula is put forward as having no alternative, as an absolute constraint. 'There is no alternative', we hear repeated *ad nauseam*. Such arrogance and deceit exclude in advance the objective necessity of fighting by means of another type of globalization: substituting the unilateral adjustment of the weak to the strong with a structural adjustment that is truly bilateral.

An alternative to capitalist globalization implies, first, the recomposition of socialist perspectives in all the different parts of the world. Socialism is not dead, but it will not be reborn through attempts to resuscitate old national social-democratic or statist Marxist-Leninist formulas or their tropical versions, all of which have been superseded. The new socialism should be much more internationalist, and at the same time contribute actively to the recomposition of regional groupings capable of opposing the internationalism of peoples to that of capital. These regional groupings as envisaged here are not the same as those conceived in the neo-imperialist logic, namely the harnessing of particular regions of the South to the central metropoles (such as the integration of Mexico into the North American Free Trade Agreement [NAFTA], the association of African countries to Europe, the reconstruction of an East Asian space dominated by Japan). On the contrary, they should bypass the constraints of the nation-state at the heart of Europe on the one hand, and on the other reinforce the power of collective negotiation and the consolidation of the regions of the Third World according to their geographical organization (Africa, Arab world, Latin America, South-East Asia). If this doesn't happen the world will return to the past, feeding uncontrollable conflicts between nations and between real or imagined communities.

Internationalization in this form would signify a moderation of the excesses of the global market, regulating the rhythm of its deployment to that of opening the way to migrations and to the construction of polycentric democratic political spaces, the necessary foundation for progressive common social policies.

Certainly the perspective of global competitiveness should never be forgotten, for it is this which roughly defines efficiency in the long term. However it remains a long-term perspective. Putting it forward as an immediate aim would be to put the cart before the horse and, in fact, reverse any chance of success. A certain protected and autocentric development is unavoidable for a long while yet. Globalization should not oppose this, but rather contribute to its success by means of a subtle organization – 'planned', even – of exchanges between the regions of the planet which are unequally developed. What I understand by a delinked and polycentric world system is nothing but this and it is within this renewed framework that North–South cooperation, and equally that of East–West, can support general progress. No miracle recipe, such as the market, can substitute for this.

What social forces could bring about such a programme? We are here concerned with producing blueprints in response to questions which only history can resolve, but of defining the terms of a lucid discussion. In this spirit one might pose the question: would national and popular alliances, operating within a democratic framework, be able to move further than the formulae of the radical populism of the 1960s? Would they be able to manage the internalized contradiction between capitalist forms of management and social forces wishing to go beyond them?

In the industrialized peripheries the articulation of these alliances around the new working class (the peasants superexploited by the burden of financing modernization, and the marginalized masses) already seems possible. Struggles played out on the real terrain of economic administration and democracy are currently engaged, as we can see in Brazil and Korea. In the Fourth World the marginalization of the productive systems brings with it the transfer of the conflict between 'the people' (mostly consisting of a reserve army on a world scale) and 'power' (whose roots in real local economic power are weak and in fact marginal) from the terrain (absent) of the true economy to that (imaginary) of 'culture', of ethnicity or religion. Here, therefore, the construction of a real alternative comes up against other important obstacles.

The question of ethnicity should be replaced in the strategic framework by an action one can sum up thus: respect diversity, unite in spite of it. Respecting diversity means renouncing the empty discourse of power which pretends to act 'in the national interest' (which this power more often than not betrays) by pretending to interiorize the ideology of the nation-state. This, then, is to accept social realities, particularly those of class, whose existence is usually denied by refusing them the means of autonomous expression – a refusal that extends to women's religious and ethnic groups. A social reality exists when individuals are conscious of it and seek a means of expressing it. A recognition of diversity, however, does not signify a crumbling away of the state by means of unlimited secessions; on the contrary, diversity should serve as a spring-board for a call to unity. This is the only perspective which would be definitively favourable to the development of popular forces. But the call to unity remains hollow if it is not associated with a denunciation of the global and local systems which, though they may not engender all the 'differences', certainly make use of them to break up the popular forces.

In all cases the problematic for the national and popular democratic alliance, as an alternative to submission to capitalist globalization, is different to that by means of which socialism has until now analysed the nature of the challenges. Underestimating the importance of polarization in world capitalism, socialist thought, in all its expressions, has defined the options open to the developing regions as either bourgeois revolution (which is supposed to make these societies follow a path exactly the same as that previously followed by the advanced capitalist societies) or socialist revolution. The thesis of polarization shows that bourgeois revolution is not a viable solution because it does not permit these societies to go beyond the boundaries of peripheral capitalism; whilst socialist revolution is not the order of the day, because the local social forces do not have sufficient maturity. Historical experience also shows that theoretically alluring palliatives believed to compensate for this lack of maturity (uninterrupted revolution or the opportunistic rosy-coloured versions of the 'non-capitalist' path) only worsen the situation created by polarization and do not eliminate the problem. The 'being caught' in the framework of capitalism and the 'historically swift' construction of socialism constitute two complementary utopia of the dominant thought, deaf to the problem of the challenge posed by polarization. The new stage of socialist thought must go beyond this.

The challenge concerns not only the countries of the periphery, because globalization has eroded the efficiency of the nation-state everywhere. This is particularly evident in Europe. The growing chaos at the heart of the EC and outside it, bears witness to this development. It can only be surmounted if a new internationalism emerges among peoples, capable of transferring the mechanisms of progressive social administration to the scheme of a new European grouping. It is in the ideological tradition of socialism that the ingredients for this response to the challenge may be found, not in the cosmopolitanism of capital, which is preoccupied with short-term profit from the differences.

Is it possible to go further? To say that the construction of a world state has become an objective historical necessity? Without doubt the rediscovery of the destruction of the planet's resources brought about by capitalist accumulation pleads in its favour. But how diminished the dominant political and cultural system looks when faced with this challenge! The arrogance of the United States is a clear demonstration. Without doubt the globalist ideology should, consistent with its premises, sustain not only the three-dimensional integration of the markets (goods and services, capital, and labour) but also envisage the complementary construction of a global state managing, in a progressive social spirit, world democracy and the resources of the planet. Obviously, the dominant liberal ideology does not do this; to the contrary, it applies itself to the weakening of states without substituting a viable alternative and without attacking the monstrous military imbalance.

In these conditions, lacking progressive social formations in each of the three parts of the world and an all-inclusive and flexible regionalization of the world system, can the United States impose the rules of the capitalist game? Which? And by what means? There is a strong temptation to encourage the conservative forces to impose the utopia of the market, which will aggravate polarization and, this being insupportable, bring with it violent eruptions. There is an urge to respond with massive bombardment, which has sadly been proven in the Gulf War.

Socialism must without doubt inscribe its strategies in the perspective of constructing a socialist world and, if not a world state, at least of a consistent political system. But it must also define the stages which will lead in this direction. In this context it seems to me that it is impossible to bypass the stage of popular national construction, of regionalization, of delinking and the building of a polycentric world.

Further Thoughts on Universalism versus Particularism and the Socialist Response to Nationalism

1. There is not much argument about the reality of what is called 'the nation'. The mere fact that most individuals say they belong to a definite nation – that is, that they consider the features, real or imaginary, which they share with their compatriots to be more decisive than any distinctions within the national group – establishes the incontestable social reality designated by that term.

Recognition of this (banal) reality does not mean at all, however, that we should give up studying its nature, limits and contradictions, and still less that we should accept the myths by which the nations in question live out their existence. For the nation is the seat of tenacious mythologies, including those which present it as a natural fact (revealing a biological perception that leads naturally to racism), whereas in fact it is a social and historical reality. Of course, the movement of society and history that led to the formation of the nations in question was not the same for each one. It is therefore necessary to stress the differences in this process because it is these which explain the profoundly divergent conceptions of the nation.

2. The concept of 'nation', like all concepts defining human communities of any kind, rests upon a fundamental contradiction between universalism (of the human species, of its destiny, and of projects for society) and particularism (of the communities that make up the human species). How do these particularisms link up with the exigencies of universalism, either to reject it or, on the contrary, to fit into or bow to it, or to lay claim to it? The task of scientific analysis is precisely to read the myths, perceptions and conceptualizations of the nation, in such a way as to lay bare this contradictory relationship.

3. The humanist concept of universalism has a history of its own, for humanity did not straightaway reach the level of abstraction required. Ethnic groups, tribes or clans – the label is of little import – lived for a long time in such separation from one another that their common human dimension had no effective and tangible social purchase. Even deities were conceived in this framework as particular to each of these particular groups.

The first great wave of what I call 'the cultural revolutions founding the tributary era' initiated the birth of the universalist concept of humanity. During the millennium or so stretching from the fifth century BC to the seventh century AD, the great religions of Zoroastrianism, Buddhism, Christianity and Islam were founded, and the great Confucian and Hellenistic philosophies were formulated. The common dimension and destiny of all human beings was thus affirmed, if only in the Beyond. To be sure, this declaration of a universalist vocation did not establish a real unification of humanity. The conditions of tributary society did not permit it, and humanity reformed itself into major tributary areas held together by their own particular universalist religion-philosophy (Christendom, Dar el Islam, the Hindu world, the Confucian world). It is still the case, however, that the tributary revolution, like all the great revolutionary moments in history, projected itself forwards and produced concepts ahead of its time.

In modern times, the bourgeois revolution started a second evolutionary wave that deepened and enriched the concept of 'universalism'. The philosophy of the Enlightenment was here the beginning of a movement that culminated in the French Revolution. As regards the concept of the nation, it defined a new content radically different from the one with which members of the tributary communities (Christendom, Islam, the Hindu or Confucian world) had experienced their lives, their membership of a community, and their perception of universalism and its limits.

The new organization of society that began to crystallize in part of Europe with the Renaissance, the conquest of the Americas and the mercantilism of the absolutist monarchies of Atlantic Europe – capitalism, to call it by its name – created an appropriate framework in the first bourgeois nation-states (England and France, in particular). But the philosophy of the Enlightenment did not divert the 'national' reality into the construction of some biological myth. On the contrary, that reality was formulated in a social (that is, not a naturalistic) vision of society. It is true that a myth was proposed for this purpose, but it was quite different from the myth of common ancestors. Rather, a 'social contract' was held to have founded the nation-state – as a state and a nation, therefore, which would not have existed without it. This concept of a social contract implied the concept of bourgeois individuality endowed with freedom.

The greatness of the French Revolution is expressed in the fact that it founded a new nation, not by reference to common blood, ancestors, or Christendom, but as 'the nation of free men' (the concept of sexual equality was not far advanced at the time) who have together made the revolution and want to live under its laws. It therefore includes all peoples who take part in it, even if (like the Alsatians) they do not express themselves in the French language. But it does not envisage that those who have not taken part (even if they are French-speaking) should belong to it as of right.

This is a nation-ideology of citizens, one might say. Logically enough, it does not hesitate to incorporate the Jews, and at its height it abolishes slavery in the colonies and raises the Blacks of San Domingo to the rank of 'citizens'. In forging the concept of 'secularism', it goes beyond religious toleration; it claims to rid the new nation of references to the past and sees Christianity as no more than a personal philosophical opinion like any other, not an element in the ideological structure of society. (The religious institution was itself thought of as an element in the tyranny of the *ancien régime*.) The declaration of 1789, which included a right to asylum and theoretically permitted any free man, whatever his origin, to declare himself a citizen of the new nation, was testimony to this ideological concept of the nation.

In this view, of course, the nation is not an affirmation of the particular against the universal; it is itself the expression of the universal. Like all great revolutions – the later Russian one, for example – it contained the project of its own extension through imitation by all peoples.

4. This said, Enlightenment thought and its product *par excellence*, the French Revolution, did not achieve their universalist objective. The capitalist system that was taking shape and expanding at the same time did not require it; and indeed, the very logic of the system defined the limits of the proposed universalism, which should be called 'bourgeois universalism', as an indication of the real interests it served.

The universalist project of the Enlightenment and the French revolution ran up against narrow historical limits in the two dimensions of the spread of capitalism:

(1) The first dimension concerns the expansion of capitalism in its European centres. This got under way not through bourgeois revolutions, as in England and France, but through the establishment of the nation-states of modern Europe. In the case of Germany, the constitution of this state was the combined result of Prussian military power and the rallying of the *ancien régime* aristocracies to the Bismarckian project, without a bourgeois revolution.

The new social hegemony that assured the spread of capitalism under these conditions could not base its legitimacy upon democratic values; it substituted 'nationalism' for them, a concept of the nation based not on the social contract but on blood descent. This 'nation of the mists' sustained itself on a founding myth that delved deep into the remote past of the Germanic tribes. Nineteenth-century German sociology even invented a term to designate this reality (or myth) of a barbarian community; it was *Gemeinschaft*. This was experienced not as a break but as a continuity, so that the religious heritage was regarded as a constituent element of the national culture.

This reactionary, almost biological conception of the nation, which culminated in Nazi racist crime, has never been extirpated from the Germanic consciousness. This explains the aberration whereby the descendant of a Schmidt who emigrated to the Volga three centuries ago is treated by German law as a German, whereas the grandson of a Turkish immigrant remains a foreigner.

The absence of a bourgeois revolution – except in England, France and Holland – meant that capitalist development in Central, Eastern and Southern Europe was built around the formation of nation-states in which the nation had supposedly (more than actually) existed prior to the constitution of the state. This movement, which I have analysed elsewhere (see Amin, *Class and Nation*) broke up the multinational empires that might have provided a no-less favourable framework for capitalist expansion. The atmosphere of triumphant nationalism created by the actual process of capitalist expansion affected in turn the old nations of democratic Western Europe, all the more so since European capitalisms were then being built within autocentred national formations at loggerheads with one another. In the resulting clash of imperialisms, mobilization of the national myth was obviously an effective weapon in the hands of the dominant classes.

Of course, there was no scientific basis for the myth of an absolute continuity of peoples; nor was there for that of a revolutionary break that would 'make a clean slate of the past', to translate from the French version of the *Internationale*. Even peoples constituted as nations, in affirming such a break, inherit from their past a number of cultural elements that are schematized in their new demands.

In France, moreover, the construction of unity had begun not in recently precipitated events, as in Germany, but in a project of the French monarchy dating back to the eleventh century. The assimilation of peoples, the progressive abandonment of local languages in favour of French, had roots in that distant past. The movement was then accelerated considerably and completed by the school system of the Republic, through which the modern French nation was built around this new, cultural-linguistic unity.

The history of Britain has some obvious similarities to that of France. The fate of the Scots, who lost the use of their language, reminds us that assimilation policies are far from being a French, Jacobin peculiarity, as many too hastily suggest. But the English bourgeois revolution of the seventeenth century, also based upon Enlightenment ideas, democratic values and the concept of a social contract, took place earlier than the French and was therefore not as radical. The break with the past was less assertive, and the compromise which retained the monarchy and aristocracy allowed a myth of continuity to survive with greater force, by boosting the retrospective value of the Magna Carta (with its feudal, non-bourgeois freedoms) and the Protestant Reformation.

Countries with a bourgeois-democratic tradition have always been inclined to conceive of the nation as a social reality open to, among other things, the assimilation of newcomers. This propensity has been reinforced whenever a country has been open to large-scale immigration.

This was the case especially in the United States, of course, but also in all the other countries of the American continent plus a number of others (Australia, for example). It has also applied to France since the late-nineteenth century, long before immigration spread throughout capitalist Europe in the 1960s. Countries with a democratic tradition reacted to this challenge in a relatively welcoming manner, with all the nuances that should be attached to this word. Either they considered the 'naturalization' of at least second-generation immigrants to be a matter of course (as in France and Britain), thereby accelerating the processes of real assimilation, or else they regarded 'incorporation' into the adopted nation (an American term expressing well the difference from 'assimilation') as the legitimate way of maintaining the original 'cultural' diversity.

A lot could be said about this last point. Defence of the American method, made fashionable by affirmations of the 'right to difference' which assimilationists deny, ignores the fact that accepted differences are also the basis for racist-type discrimination and hierarchization between the 'communities' in question, which, in the case of the United States, have roots in slavery and in scornful attitudes to non-Anglo-Saxons. Although there can be no denying the right to be different, it is no less important to defend the 'right to be similar'. Ill-considered praise of difference often conceals a misty concept of culture, whose ostensibly unchanging specificity allows it to substitute for biology, whereas real history displays, on the contrary, the malleability of cultures.

(2) The second dimension defining the limits of bourgeois universalism concerns the expansion of capitalism in its Asian and African peripheries. There was never any question of extending to these colonies the democratic values of the Enlightenment, whether democratic political rights or even (in the case of France) the concepts of secularism and assimilation. Contrary to the legend that the Islamicists propagate in Algeria, for example, the colonial authorities were careful to avoid extending French law to their Muslim subjects; indeed, they scrupulously respected the *sharia* (law) which in a very few respects (especially regarding the status of women) was challenged by the FLN when it came to power, rather than by the French colonialists!

The truncated character of the universalism offered by capitalism is no cause for surprise. It was a necessary and logical concomitant of the centre/periphery distinction inherent in the world expansion of capitalism, whose economic and social dimensions tend to polarize by their very nature.

As a world system, therefore, actually existing capitalism left the peripheries out of the field of operation of the values promoting universalism. The socialist and national-liberation movements were left to face this major challenge.

5. Socialism was confronted with nationalism first in nineteenth-century Europe, and later in the context of the colonial question.

The least that can be said here is that socialist thought, in all its expressions, always situated itself within, never short of, the Enlightenment tradition. The historical socialist Left was defined by profoundly democratic convictions, whereas the Right was always inclined to limit democratic freedoms when these threatened class privileges. The Left and socialism have always felt a sense of indignation at nationalist discourse, particularly of the biological-communalist variety. Socialism has always set itself the goal of strengthening the consciousness and solidarity of the working classes, against the devastating effects of the nationalist ideologies manipulated by the exploiting classes.

The errors, blind-spots and limitations of socialism must be placed in this context. Most often, they are the result of over-optimism either about the capacities of peoples to rid themselves of the reactionary ideas of the past or about the progress made in advancing socialism's demands. For example, all socialists (including Marxists) have tended to overestimate the historical courage of the bourgeoisie, to believe it capable of breaking down the obstacles that nations might pose to the expansion of capitalism (capable, that is, of imposing market integration in every dimension, even that of the world labour market).

I have stressed this point because the truncated character of the world market – its exclusion of labour – underlies the polarization intrinsic to capitalism and defines the insuperable limits of both the bourgeoisie and the capitalist system. The errors of the socialist movement regarding the colonial question have their origin here.

Trusting in progress and overestimating the capacities of capitalism, socialists have tended to believe that its expansion would gradually erase national boundaries, and that the resulting worldwide homogenization of society would lay the basis for class struggle and socialism at a world level. They have therefore also tended to favour strategies likely to accelerate evolution in that direction, while advocating the most democratic possible means of reaching the goal. Hence they have been inclined to prefer assimilation, by democratic means, over the defence of specificities and differences, which they have often seen as vestiges of a dying past.

I highlight this dimension of socialist thought because it is today questioned by the stress on the right to difference. Although the currents which promote this have sincerely democratic intentions, especially within the Anglo-American and Nordic traditions, it still remains an ambivalent stress. For, as I have already indicated, difference has often been the basis of discrimination, and recognition of its legitimacy a way of dressing up unavowed racism. The demand does not, then, mark an indisputable advance of the democratic spirit; it also reflects the seeping of dominant conservative ideas into the history of the societies of Northern Europe.

Faced with the reality of national identities, yet concerned to insist upon class interests, socialists have defended positions which, though not always politically effective in the short term, have been noble, worthy and in advance of the times. I am thinking here of the attitudes of the socialist movement within the multinational empires of Europe: the Austro-Marxists of the Austro-Hungarian Empire, and the Bolsheviks of the Russian Empire. The Austro-Marxists wanted to save the large state, but by reconstructing it on the basis of recognition of ethnic, religious and national differences as democratically legitimate. The Bolsheviks, and the Third International after them, went further still in this direction. They made the maximum possible concessions to national facts, or what were said to be facts, and conceived the idea of a multinational socialist state. Their actual practice in this respect is certainly a theme for analysis and criticism.

The Constitution of the USSR, like that of Yugoslavia which followed its lead, is not just an historical document but reflects experiences that were lived in all their contradictory reality. The socialism of the Third International was in this sense the extreme inheritor of radical democratic thought; it even pushed its logic to dangerous extremes. Almost extravagantly respectful of the right to difference, Bolshevism did not simply proclaim the right of nations to self-determination; it blocked any possible evolution by writing the political federation of nations into the constitutions of both the USSR and Yugoslavia.

The reality of these two countries is complex: in the USSR, there was doubtless Russian cultural domination but also a redistribution of wealth to the ex-colonial periphery such as capitalist imperialism never practised; and in Yugoslavia there was equal distribution among Serbs, Croats and others. But whatever the true situation may have been, the ideological perceptions common to the Third International carried the legitimation of difference beyond what was necessary.

Capitalism, through the planing-down effects of the market, would in this respect have been infinitely less cautious than the communist regimes that were concerned to save cultures from market-planning and eventual oblivion. Today, socialism is paying dearly for that excess of democratic respect for difference, which it helped to keep alive. In Yugoslavia, for instance, a large and growing part of the new generations no longer recognized itself in the 'historic nations' of the Constitution, and declared its 'Yugoslav' nationality. But the internally and externally dominant forces, instead of supporting this trend, tried to breathe fresh life into national identities that were being left behind. This reactionary option of the Yugoslav dominant classes, and of the forces that supported them in Europe, thus bears a major responsibility in the ensuing involution and the wild explosion of criminal chauvinisms with which we are familiar.

The ideas of the Russian Revolution, like those of the French before it, were ahead of what objectively needed to be done in response to the problems of Russia and the Russian Empire. This was true of the right to difference up to and including secession, but also of the shared, universalist objective of constructing a socialist humanity.

6. Historical socialism therefore developed a vision in advance of its time to meet the challenges of nationalism as it might manifest itself in Europe. Faced with the problems of the Asian and African peripheries, however, socialism found itself pretty well powerless. The history of the epochs preceding capitalism, the results of integration in the modern capitalist system, the challenges with which these societies were confronted – all this largely went beyond the resources of a classical socialist thought with Eurocentrist origins.

In the peripheral regions of the system, capitalist expansion gave rise to complex social formations. It produced a great variety of situations, in which the national or ethnic factor often assumes a position different from the one that it occupies in the central modes of capitalist expansion.

Through a Eurocentrist simplification that I have criticized elsewhere, attempts have often been made to project the European experience – its distinctive feudalism, with the dispersion of political power and a later concomitance between capitalist expansion and the constitution of 'the modern nations' – onto the different realities of Asia and Africa. By contrast, I have underlined the following factors in the worlds of the capitalist periphery:

(1) The highly diverse models of the tributary system dominating humanity in precapitalist epochs; the existence of a full-fledged

tributary model characterized in some cases by a strong centralization of political power (China and Egypt, for example); the combination of this model in other cases with developed trade relations (the Arab-Islamic world, for example).

(2) The existence, in these conditions, of nations preceding capitalism, which, in the case of strong political centralization, assured centralization and redistribution of the tributary surplus (China, Egypt and, in some periods, the Arab world), as opposed to ethnic fragmentation in other cases (sub-Saharan Africa, for example).

(3) The importance of the cultural dimension in defining each of the great areas that made up the precapitalist tributary world (European Christendom, Dar el Islam, the Hindu constellation, the Confucian world); and the more pronounced survival of manifestations of tributary ideological dominance in the peripheries of the world-capitalist system, which have not experienced a radical ideological and cultural break such as the Renaissance or the Enlightenment in Europe.

In these circumstances, the complex social reality inevitably eluded the ethnocentrist analyses dominant in modern bourgeois thought and also, to a large extent, in socialist thought. The Second International, in this respect inheriting and scarcely moving beyond bourgeois Enlightenment thinking, shared with the bourgeois defenders of capitalism (democratic or not) the illusion that capitalist expansion would eventually erase all specificities, understood as vestiges in the course of disappearance. It thus legitimized its rallying to the defence of colonialism and imperialism, as 'objective factors of progress' (see Bill Warren's *Imperialism, Pioneer of Capitalism*, for example). In doing so, it failed to see what I regard as essential in an analysis of capitalism: namely, the inherently polarizing character of world capitalist expansion. The Third International, for its part, broke with this ethnocentrist tradition and placed anti-imperialism at the heart of its strategies for struggle. The simplifications this sometimes involved should not make us forget the positive character of the break, which made possible a more correct analysis of what was at stake, as well as a development of more effective liberation strategies.

Whatever we make of their theoretical conceptions – prejudices and blind-spots or, on the contrary, breakthroughs allowing forward movement – the national liberation movements of the modern capitalist periphery were faced with realities that could not simply be reduced either to the clash of the basic class interests defining the capitalist mode of production (conflict between bourgeoisie and proletariat) or to a struggle by supposedly pre-existing nations to achieve their objective of liberation. The national liberation movements were forced to be sufficiently realistic to reject the simplifying visions purveyed by the dominant Eurocentrism.

On the question of the nation, the national liberation movements therefore opted directly and instinctively for the perspective emphasizing the unity of peoples in struggle against imperialism. Beyond the horizons of ethnicity or of religious and other communities, they pleaded for the construction, or reconstruction, of large states, old or new. They were certainly not wrong in this choice, and their accusations that imperialism always promoted division were not without foundation. Today one tends to forget the reality of this: the English deployed all their resources to break Indian unity (and eventually managed to separate off Muslim India, while failing in their attempts to break the unity of the nations of Hindu India); the French and the English played the cards of African balkanization all right, as they did in the Middle East, and so on.

This being said, the concepts invoked by the national liberation movements to legitimate their option for unity varied considerably from one current to another. On the Right, in conservative nationalist minds, the 'nation' in whose name people were called to the struggle remained mythical or shrouded in mist; sometimes it flew in the face of the ethnic, religious or linguistic diversity of its constituent parts. These dominant cultural affiliations were similarly nebulous in definitions of the earlier tributary systems – Hinduism or Islam, for example. And the definition of a transethnic 'new nation' in sub-Saharan Africa was largely mythical, as if Senegalese, Nigerian or Zairian nationality cancelled out Wolof or Diola, Ibo, Yoruba or Hausa, Bakongo or Baluba ethnicity.

In one way or another, then, right-wing ideologies within the national liberation movement, expressing the aims of the national bourgeoisies, were predisposed to join up with the misty philosophies of nationalism produced in backward Europe, the Europe that did not participate in the Enlightenment.

The ideology of the Arab 'nationalists' (the *qawmiyin*) is an exemplary illustration of this. The 'Arab nation' is here conceived not as a complex, evolving product of history, but as an intrinsic, quasi-biological essence: hence 'Arabness' (*al uruba*) on the model of 'Germanness'. A mythological conception of this kind leaves the way open to confusion, between Arabness and Islam, for example. One finds many proofs of such confusion in modern *qawmiyin* discourse ('Islam is an inseparable component of Arabness', etc.); they facilitated the later turn to religious fundamentalism, occupying the ground abandoned after the failure of the strategies of Arab nationalism (which really did fail in their attempts to forge Arab unity). In the Third World today, this rather nebulous type of discourse – no more so, though, than that of European nationalisms – is certainly not peculiar to the Arabs. The discourse of negritude, for example, is no different in nature.

Nevertheless, it would be wrong to reduce the discourses of the nation within the liberation movement to the nebulous concept just called into question. The left wing of the movement, including its communist part, has always drawn its inspiration from the philosophy of the Enlightenment. In a genuinely democratic spirit, this Left has always upheld respect for local identities, for linguistic or religious minorities, and so on. It has tried to make unity prevail, but without denying the diversity of its components.

Whether legitimized mythologically or democratically, the principle of unity has not been a hollow and deceitful slogan; more often than not, it has actually been a positive and progressive reality. This allows us to say that, on the whole, the ruling classes in the states deriving from decolonization have been transethnic or panethnic. This has been the case especially in India and sub-Saharan Africa.

The postwar erosion of the national-bourgeois project, which I call the Bandung Project, is at the root of the collapse of the concept of multi-ethnic nationalism, and of the emergence of a new ethnicism which, as I have written elsewhere, has set out to take the nations by storm. (This phrase reproduces the title in French of my book *L'Ethnie à l'assaut des Nations*, L'Harmattan, Paris, 1994.)

The mechanism of this present crisis of the state is nearly everywhere the same. It involves a sweeping reduction in the surplus available to the ruling class, a surplus which used to allow that class to keep expanding through absorption of those who benefited from economic growth and new possibilities of social ascent. Now the sudden cut in surplus margins deprives the ruling class of its ability to assure development, and hence of the legitimacy that used to ground its power. The unity of this class is breaking down, and its elements presently at bay are seeking to base a new legitimacy, whenever possible, upon such aspects as ethnicity.

Africa is not the only region where such phenomena are unfolding before our eyes: India, the former Yugoslavia and the former Soviet Union are other examples. The re-emergence of ethnicity is not due, then, to a kind of atavism noisily manifesting itself in a series of explosions spaced out over time but rather to the strategies deployed by a ruling class at bay, whether the nomenclature of Eastern Europe, or the privileged classes of such regions of the Third World as India or

Africa.

7. I will now try briefly to draw together the threads from these lengthy reflections.

Deepening globalization put an end to the postwar (1945–90) international order, but this did not mean that the fundamental contradiction of capitalism – understood as an essentially polarizing global system – was about to be overcome. The real challenge now facing humanity is to build a new world society upon principles which allow the disastrous effects of such polarization to be gradually erased. This goal, which involves perfecting the universalism initiated by capitalism, presents in turn a troubling challenge to the concept of the nation. For it implies that this concept has to be shifted in a humanist and democratic direction capable of responding to the contradiction between specificity and universalism.

Initiated by the great universal ideologies-cum-religions of the tributary epochs, deepened by the philosophy of the Enlightenment, and reinterpreted by the socialist movement, the response to the challenge must now be carried to a higher qualitative level that corresponds to the advances of globalization.

Unfortunately, the profound crisis through which the collapse of the old order finds expression involves a disarray that sets up disastrous processes of involution. These barbaric and ultimately racist reactions are defined by a revival of nebulous interpretations of the nation, various forms of ethnicism, uncritical rehabilitation of specificity, and all manner of communalist introversion. 'Respect for difference' and democratic rights, understood in a formal and impoverished sense, must not become a pretext for legitimizing this involution, which must be combated squarely, and more human, and, in the end, more effective responses must gradually be advanced.

Political action programmes liable to achieve this will require an enrichment of the concept and practices of democracy so that it respects difference but also upholds the 'right to be similar'. Such programmes will also require a concrete notion of the stages that need to be gone through in this universalist perspective. The stage of constructing big regional entities in the various historic areas (Europe, ex-USSR, Latin America, the Arab world, sub-Saharan Africa, India, China, South-East Asia) is probably a necessary transition, the most effective response at this point to the contradiction between specificity and universalism.

References

Amin, Samir, *Class and Nation, Historically and in the Current Crisis*, Monthly Review Press, NY, 1980, Chpter 5

Amin, Samir, *Empire of Chaos*, Monthly Review Press, New York, 1993

Amin, Samir, *Maldevelopment: Anatomy of a Global Failure*, Zed Books, 1990

Amir, Samir, *Les enjeux stratégiques en Méditerranée*, Première Patrie, L'Harmattan, Paris, 1992

Mukherjee, Ramkrishna, *The Rise and Fall of the East India Company*, Monthly Review Press, New York, 1976

Warren, Bill, *Imperialism, Pioneer of Capitalism*, London, 1980

CHAPTER 5

What are the Conditions for Relaunching Development in the South?

Development off the Agenda

Development is off the agenda: the governments of the West are preoccupied with 'crisis management'; the countries of former Eastern Europe are converting to market capitalism; and Latin America, Africa and the Arab world are concerned primarily with the servicing of external debt. Only the developing countries of Asia – China, East (Taiwan, Korea) and South-East Asia and more modestly, India – continue to be preoccupied with sustaining an accelerated rate of economic growth.

For the first three post-Second World War decades, 'development' was the major preoccupation of all regimes. Three major projects were implemented with considerable success: (i) the welfare state in the developed West; (ii) Sovietism in the East; (iii) accelerated modernization in the non-aligned countries of the Bandung group of Asia and Africa, and Latin America ('developmentalism'). All three of these projects either unfolded within the framework of autocentric national economies or, in the case of the countries of the East and the South, aspired to construct such autocentric economies. They differed in their relationship ('interdependence') with the world economy: Atlantism, the construction of Europe, in the case of the developed countries of the West; a 'negotiated' opening to the world economy in the case of the countries of the South; quasi-autarky for the countries of the East. They differed also with regard to the nature of the social forces driving the project in question (historic social-democratic compromise of capital and labour within the nation-states of the West; populism with Marxist or socialist pretensions in the South); and differed also with respect to political systems (for example, electoral pluralism, one-party states). The diversity of differences, due to the incontestable variety of historical legacies, and the fact that some countries were more and others less egalitarian in terms of income distribution, should not detract from the profound similarity of objectives: the increase in material welfare by economic development, and the strengthening of the nation within the world.

In the course of the thirty 'golden years' of postwar growth, the internationalization of the world economy (whether encouraged or resisted) progressively eroded the capacity of the state to manage modernization, while new dimensions of the problem asserted themselves (for example, environmental degradation on a planetary scale). In 1968–71, the world system entered a phase of structural crisis, which continues to this day. The crisis manifests itself in the return of high and persistent unemployment accompanied by a slowing down of growth in the West, the collapse of Sovietism, and serious regression in some regions of the Third World, accompanied by unsustainable levels of external indebtedness. By contrast, East Asia took off into accelerated economic growth.

The postwar era (1945–90) was characterized by serious conflicts between different parts of the world: the West–East Cold War; and conflicts of the Western bloc with the Bandung powers. Nevertheless, there was generalized economic development, in some ways more rapid in the East and the South, giving rise to the idea that it was possible to catch up with the developed countries.

In fact, the strong growth of the age world economy was the product of political developments which favoured poor nations and the popular classes in a general way, to the detriment of the unilateral logic of capital. I insist on this fact, generally overlooked or ignored in (partial) explanations of the 'boom' (or the booms). The defeat of fascism contained and limited power relations within all the societies of the world, and between them.

In the West it created power relations significantly more favourable to the working classes than ever before in the entire history of capitalism. These new relations of power are the key to the understanding of the 'welfare state', an historic compromise between capital and labour which the French regulation school has called 'Fordism' (a questionable designation because Fordism was introduced in the United States before, and in opposition to, the Roosevelt New Deal). I have insisted on the fundamental importance of this political factor, underestimated in the dominant analyses, which suggest that capital sought – naturally, so to speak – a compromise with labour. The victory of the Soviet Union and the Chinese revolution created internal and international conditions favouring the development of the countries of the East, and also those of the West, in so far as they contributed to pressures exerted on capital to engage in the historic social-democratic compromise. Debates concerning the social nature of these developments – were they or were they not socialist? – and the role of the internal contradictions resulting in the exhaustion and eventual collapse of the historic compromise, should not deflect attention from the positive effects of West–East political competition, reinforced by US military expenditures. The simultaneous rise of national liberation movements in the Third World and the ability of postcolonial regimes to harness the benefits of East–West competition favoured economic growth in the South in a number of ways.

The three pillars erected in the wake of the victory against fascism, and which sustained development in the thirty golden years, have been progressively eroded by the limitations inherent in the class relations upon which they rested: the limitations of the social-democratic compromise; and the ambitions of the Soviet bourgeoisies and those of the Third World. These internal contradictions, manifested in policies which undermined the logic of national economic development, and fed by trends of ever-increasing globalization, lie at the root of the brutal reversal of the political conjuncture of the 1980s. Briefly outlined above, the collapse of the three post-Second World War projects has terminated what I call 'the postwar anti-fascist era', in which capital was constrained to operate within structures relatively favourable to the peoples of the world.

Over the past three decades, conditions favourable to the reconstruction of the logic of unilateral capital were recreated. But the logic of unilateral capital cannot, by and of itself, generate growth, much less development (strong growth, accompanied by full employment and income distribution favouring the popular classes). Based on the exclusive search for the highest financial returns, it tends instead to produce an unequal distribution of income between social classes, domestically and internationally, which contributes to relative economic stagnation. Marx and Keynes stand alone in having understood the deflationist logic of unilateral capital, a lesson forgotten by the progressive eradication of the anti-fascist spirit in the postwar years.

Contemporary Society is in Crisis, but there is Not Yet a Crisis of Capitalism

Contemporary society is manifestly in crisis, if we define crisis as a situation in which the expectations of the majority cannot be satisfied by the logic of the system. People want such things as full employment, improvement in social services and opportunities for social mobility. The unilateral logic of capital produces unemployment, impoverishment and marginalization. Nations want independence and dignity; the logic of global capital produces the opposite. In this process, states and governments have lost the legitimacy which enabled them to intervene in the regulation of social relations in favour of the popular classes, and to defend their national interests on the international scene. Western democracy, Sovietism (vulgarly referred to as 'communism' by its opponents) and the national populism of Bandung are all three in crisis. To speak of the 'crisis of capitalism', however, is something else. The expression has no meaning until such time as the popular social forces opposed to the logic of capital have coherent and feasible counter-projects, as was the case in the anti-fascist postwar years.

The political forces which have arisen in the wake of the collapse of the postwar order have been placed almost at the service of the logic of the deployment of capital.

I have analysed in some detail policies of what I have called 'crisis management'. Capitalism and crisis are not incompatible: far from it, because the logic of capital necessarily generates crisis. Left to itself, capital can manage the crisis, but cannot resolve it.

Crisis results from the fact that the profits of capitalist exploitation cannot find sufficient financially profitable new outlets capable of expanding productive capacity. The management of the crisis consists of finding alternative new investments for excess short-term capital, in order to avert a massive and brutal collapse of the financial system, as happened in the 1930s. The solution, by contrast, implies a modification of the rules of the game affecting income distribution, consumption, and investment decisions, in other words, an alternative social project to that funded exclusively on profitability criteria. There will be no solution to the crisis unless and until the anti-systemic social forces impose constraints on capital which are exterior to and independent of the logic of pure capital.

Crisis management by national governments proceeds by policies of deregulation designed both to weaken the rigidities of trade unionism and dismantle and liberalize prices and wages; reduce public expenditure (principally subsidies and social services); and privatize and liberalize external transactions. The recipe is the same for all governments and its justification is based on the same vague and excessive dogmatisms: liberalization frees potential initiatives stifled by interventionism and puts the engine of economic growth back on the rails; those who liberalize fastest and most completely will become more competitive in open world markets. But as Marx and Keynes understood so clearly, such liberalization will ensnare the economy into deflationist spirals of stagnation, unmanageable at the international level, multiplying conflicts which cannot be mediated, against the empty promise of future 'healthy' development. On what basis, with what criteria can these policies be judged or evaluated? Nobody knows. At the same time, the legitimation of choice is reinforced by political and ideological propositions which are as vague, and false, as those advanced concerning economic mechanisms. Economic liberalization is presented as synonymous with political democracy and all critiques of these policies are held to be democratically inadmissible. The merits of economic liberalism are praised in the name of 'transparency', the state being considered, by definition, as the locus of opacity (ignoring the fact that the democratic state provides the best conditions for transparency), while in fact the – very real – opacity of private business protected by 'business confidentiality' escapes even a passing mention. The social and economic realities of oligopolies, the privileged relations of the private with the public sector, and corruption, are not the object of scientific analysis. Rarely have we witnessed an ideological discourse as extreme as any dogmatic fundamentalism, repeated incessantly by the media and the dominant discourse, as if it were based on established evidence.

The globalization of capital requires a regime of crisis management, such as we have here described. Enormous volumes of short-term capital require the subordination of economic mechanisms to unadulterated private profitability criteria. Liberalization of international capital movements, floating exchange rates, high rates of interest, American balance-of-payments deficits, Third World indebtedness, and privatization constitute a perfectly rational set of conditions which offer global capital the possibility of speculative financial profits, to avoid the danger of a massive devaluation. To gain some idea of the enormity of the excess volumes of financial capital, we compare the annual value of world trade, which is in the region of US$3000 billion, with international capital flows of about US$80,000 to 100,000 billion, 30 times larger. I refer the reader to a previous analysis of the rationality of this set of crisis management policies. I have drawn attention to the fact that they are perfectly rational and efficient from this point of view, because the literature critiquing liberalization policies, more often than not, treats each measure in isolation, and finds them to be apparently absurd.

From the perspectives of crisis management, the international institutions are instruments in the service of the regulation of West–South and West–East relations. In this context, the function of the IMF and the World Bank, and also GATT, masquerading behind the discourse of free trade, is the protection of market control by the dominant transnational oligopolies. The G7 try to coordinate these crisis management policies, with no attempt to address either the basic problems of the crisis, nor the conflict of interest between the principal partners which contribute to it.

Solutions: Liberalism without Borders?

The priority given to the demands of managing the crisis created by the uncontested triumph of the rule of private profit are taking us no nearer to a solution. On the contrary, each day takes us further away from a solution. The crisis, which is now 20 years old, started at the end of the 1960s and the opening of the 1970s (before the first oil shock) with a progressive decline in the level of productive investment, and the growth of a mass of excess financial capital which has not ceased to increase ever since. Ignoring the persistence and tenacity of economic stagnation, successive governments continue to use the language of conjunctural 'recessions' and 'recoveries', when in fact we have a fundamental structural disequilibrium resulting from the triumph of economic liberalism.

The resulting social catastrophe has hit all regions of the world. In the developed centres it is manifested in permanent unemployment; in the peripheries, in the blockage of economic growth and the aggravation of impoverishment and societal regression. At the global level, measures which should have been deployed to save the future of the planet have been sacrificed. The ideology of the dominant discourse, however, presents all these disasters as temporary measures required for the re-launching of development. In reality unilateral subordination to the laws of profit fatally traps countries into deflationary spirals with no possibility of independent exit. The reversal, when it comes, is always the product of a shock external to the unilateral logic of capital. The modification of social relations in favour of a redistribution of income, preparations for war, or the geographic opening of colonial expansion, create the conditions favourable to renewed economic expansion able to sustain a wave of technological renewal. It was in this way that the strengthening of the position of the working classes which accompanied the anti-fascist victory created the conditions for the expansion of mass-production industries after the war. Popular interpretations which explain the postwar Fordist regime in terms of this wave of innovations invert the direction of causality. I side with Paul Sweezy and others in holding the (minority) view that this is how capitalism has historically overcome its natural tendency to stagnation.

We cannot escape the crisis by following policies of 'liberalism without borders'. This is a utopia, tenaciously held throughout the history of capitalism because it expresses in extreme form the hardcore ideological vision of a pure capitalism reduced to the laws of accumulation and guided exclusively by the strict logic of capital.

Total liberalism has never existed and historical moments which approximate the political condition for its institution have always been brief. This is because extreme liberalism necessarily produces a political reaction to check, limit or modify political and social relations, thus creating the conditions for a new phase of expansion, or for war. The ideologues of liberalism are incapable of understanding this.

The postwar expansion lasted four decades before exhausting the possibilities presented by the social systems constructed on the basis of the anti-fascist victory. The project of the liberal utopia has brought us to catastrophe in a far shorter time.

Nationalism

Attempts to institute utopian liberal projects have always produced political reactions of rejection. These rarely take the form of a systematic counterproject, coherent and potentially effective in solving the crisis. In the first instance, they are almost always spontaneous, partial, contradictory, and even conflictual. Today, in a global system characterized by profound internationalization, in the form they take they may be described as protectionist: the partial closure of borders; control of capital movements; measures to defend domestic industries and the property of nationals; in some cases the return to the social contract of labour and capital; and the restoration of state intervention.

Such reactions find legitimation in the renewal of the discourse of nationalism, which passes easily into chauvinism, aggressive in the case of the relatively strong, defensive in the case of the weak.

Nationalist policies are not necessarily inefficient, as claimed by the liberal theoretical discourse. If Asia has, until now, escaped general crisis, and high rates of growth have prevailed in Japan, Korea and Taiwan, with accelerated growth in China and also in South-East Asia and India, albeit at lower rates, how do we explain this exception? The reasons are undoubtedly many and complex, and vary from one country to another in this region which comprises over half of humanity, because social systems and levels of historic development are different in different countries. All manner of possible explanations have been offered, including some which accord pride of place to cultural factors, real or imaginary, as illustrated by the debate concerning Confucianism. I simply draw attention to the fact that all the countries in question have, to one degree or another, adopted policies marked by strong economic nationalism, in the protectionist and statist sense noted above. They have not, like the countries of the EC, the United States, Latin America or Africa, followed the policy prescriptions of liberalism. They have, in fact, done the opposite, whether we look at Japan, an advanced capitalist country, Korea, in rapid construction, the market socialism of Deng Xiaoping's China, or the more integrated Third World capitalist countries of South-East Asia and India.

From initial levels of development more or less the same, impressive results have been achieved, in accordance with the degree to which nationalist policies of protectionism and statism were systematic and coherent. Why were these countries able to choose such policies and to implement them? The complex reasons are connected with the geostrategic preoccupations of the United States in the region (exceptional support extended to Japan, Korea, Taiwan and South-East Asia in exchange for their participation in the anti-communist crusade, resulting in a tolerance for nationalism not permitted elsewhere), the sheer size of the continental countries of China and India where the expansion of internal markets is always an option in the event of export problems (although other large countries such as Brazil and the new Russia appear either unwilling or unable to mobilize their large domestic markets to their advantage), the particularities of social structures (if China did better than India it is surely because Maoism set in motion a gigantic social transformation which formed the foundation for later economic growth), and perhaps other (cultural) reasons also. None of the countries of the region, with the qualified exception of India, is particularly respectful of democracy. Japan resembles a one-party political model more than the pluralist Western one, and all the regimes of East and South-East Asia are, as far as one can tell, authoritarian.

Are these nationalistic practices capable of protecting the Asian region indefinitely? This is difficult to say. Japan, and perhaps also the medium-sized countries of East and South-East Asia might be threatened. India is in a political crisis which threatens economic stability. China remains a potential exception, if it can prevent its southern provinces, attracted by the Korea-Taiwan-Hong Kong model, from endangering national unity. (An alternative policy would be to direct the growth of these provinces toward the development of the interior of the country.) But the growing economic interpenetration within the entire region gives Asia a relative measure of autonomy with respect to the rest of the world. This constitutes a factor favourable to the continued pursuit of the 'Asian miracle'.

But if nationalism in Asia has produced positive results in terms of economic growth (although not in social justice or democratization), this is not the case in other regions of the world hit by the crisis.

The Dangers of Anti-Democratic Regression: The Ethnic Assault, Religious Fundamentalism and Neo-Fascism

In Latin America, sub-Saharan Africa and the Arab world, the developmental nationalism of the Bandung years is a matter of the past. The retreat has not provided a way of moving beyond these policies. On the contrary, it has resulted in serious regression. I have suggested that we should interpret the ethnic assault on the nation (here as in Eastern Europe and the former USSR), and the illusions of religious fundamentalism (principally Islamic, but also Hindu) as manifestations of this regression. Far from opening the way to the democratization of states and societies, and a renewal of a positive nationalism and regional cooperation, these involutions raise the possibility of a kind of neo-fascism of weak countries.

In Latin America, the reactions are possibly less negative, in so far as democratic forces appear to be more solid. But can they articulate a coherent project of social progress, which must necessarily embrace, here as elsewhere, a healthy dose of nationalism (that is, the rejection of the polarizing capitalist globalization of the liberal utopia) and a commitment to regional cooperation?

In Europe, we cannot exclude the possibility of a return to nationalism, in reaction to the European liberal project. Reduced to the concept of the common market, that project carries within it a contradiction which threatens to be fatal. European economic integration cannot be irreversible until accompanied by political integration based on a new social contract between capital and labour, which can only be brought into being by a coherent Left on an all-European scale. Implemented by the Right, the European project is today visibly in danger of sinking, if not actually exploding by the force of nationalist backfire. The second best of a German Europe offers no way out of the problem. But these right-wing nationalisms which encourage the rehabilitation of fascism will in the course of time generate a renewal of progressive social reaction. Operating within a system which remains based largely on the principles of liberalism, this suggests a continuing cycle of action/reaction, encasing the continent in a regressive economic, political and ideological spiral. This cannot constitute an effective response to the crisis, given the degree of globalization attained by the economies of the region. In Eastern Europe and in the former Soviet Union the impasses within which the rise of nationalisms and sub-nationalisms have enmeshed the societies are even more dramatic.

Established powers here and there, in the United States, in Europe, in the former East and the Soviet Union, in Latin America, Africa and the Middle East, are first and foremost preoccupied with the management of the political crisis, itself produced by the economic crisis. But political crisis management is no more effective in bringing about long-term solutions than is its economic counterpart. I have characterized the political crisis as 'chaos': the impasse of the EU and possible involutions; dramatic chaos and disarticulation in Eastern Europe and the former USSR; and the collapse of a number of societies in the Third World. The political management of this chaos is based on cynical practices of short-term *realpolitik*, the manipulation of nationalisms, culturalisms, racisms and ethnicities leading to fascism. In East Europe, Latin America, Africa and the Middle East, these policies consist of throwing oil on the fires in the hope of gaining a short-term advantage by weakening regional powers and reducing the chances of a progressive renaissance of the societies in question. In this spirit, I have suggested a critical re-reading of the policies of crisis management in terms of their military (low-intensity warfare) as well as political dimensions, in particular as they have affected Yugoslavia, Ethiopia, East Europe, Africa and the Middle East.

Far from serving the objectives of the dominant discourse which claims that democratization is on the rise, the economic and political management of the crisis has everywhere reinforced the danger of anti-democratic regression. Liberalism engenders the risk of fascism, as Karl Polanyi showed in his analysis, *The Great Transformation* (1944), in which he invited his contemporaries to understand that the victory of anti-fascism and the rejection of utopian liberal policies which characterized the era following the end of the First World War could create the conditions for a new economic expansion. The lesson, now forgotten, must be recalled with force. We cannot escape the crisis and the risks of regression to fascism without breaking categorically with the logic of neoliberal globalization.

History does not repeat itself, at least not in the same manner. The term 'fascism' carries abusive connotations from experiences of another era, which is different from our own. Nevertheless neofascism, as I will call it, shares with its fascist ancestor anti-democratic characteristics and common methods. In the developed countries of the centre it does not have to take the form of a big stick as advocated by the fringe movements (such as racism) for the unilateral imposition of policies favouring big capital (and in this manner perpetuating the crisis and the management of marginalization in the form of an economy of multiple speeds, as is naïvely acknowledged). But even here, slippage toward the old model of national fascism and chauvinism is not excluded, free from closer observation by the preservation of forms of electoral democracy, manipulated and void of all real content. The danger of the rehabilitation of fascism should not be underestimated. In the countries of the periphery, situated in what P. G. Casanova so well described as 'global colonialism', neofascism is the more brutal the weaker and more hopeless the societies in which it operates. Ethnic cleansing and the carving up of states, terrorist dictatorships in the name of regional unities, already apparent, are forms taken by local powers unable to resist the submission of their societies to the globalized economy. These practices may perpetuate the appearance of order favourable to the exploitation of these peoples by dominant world capital, and for this reason, be supported by external powers.

Reflections on a Counter-Project: Some Basic Propositions

Neither the persistence of the liberal nor the logic of neofascist rejection offers escape from the infernal circle of crisis and chaos.

An effective response to these challenges is not possible until the lessons of Polanyi's 'Great Transformation' have been learned. History is not shaped by the infallible laws of pure economics, as believed by some university professors. It is the product of social reactions to the effects of these laws, which in turn define the social relations of the framework within which economic laws operate. It is the anti-systemic force of an organized, coherent and effective refusal to subordinate society to the unilateral and absolute needs of economic laws (in this context the laws of capitalist profiteering) which in reality give shape to history, rather than any logic inherent in the accumulation of capital. These forces determine the possibilities and the forms of expansion deployed within the institutional framework which they impose on economic and social organization.

The method advocated here does not permit us to formulate ready-made methods of escaping from the crisis. Solutions can only come as a result of transformations of the relations of social and political forces resulting from struggles where outcomes are unpredictable. We can, however, offer reflections on coherent and feasible counter-projects. In this way we might prevent social movements from becoming sidetracked into the impasse of false (neofascist) solutions. I thus limit myself to some basic propositions concerning such reflections.

Although the world cannot be managed as a single market, and ideological and political intervention cannot be eliminated in favour of unilateral submission to the market's supposed laws (as believed by anti-statist ideologues), the fact of globalization cannot simply be ignored or denied. It is not possible to turn the clock back on the course of history. A return to the postwar model of economic expansion, based on the central position occupied by the autocentric nation-state in economic, political and cultural affairs, implies economic and other untenable regressions. This is why backward-looking ideologies which deny the irreversible nature of the evolutionary trajectory will inevitably be called upon to function like fascisms, that is to say they will serve the needs of the new conditions of globalization, while pretending to offer escape and liberation. They are based on deception and lies and this is why they cannot function without the authoritarian negation of democracy. They are constrained to mobilize societies on the basis of false problems – for example, ethnic purity, submission to supposed laws of religion – and to use these false causes as instruments to impose their dictatorships by terror.

The challenge thus consists of reconciling the interdependence implied by globalization and the inequalities of power of the social partners (workers in different sectors of the economy, some more competitive than others) and the national partners (dominant centres, middle powers, industrialized peripheries, the marginalized Fourth World) in relation to global capital. Let us start with some self-evident banalities: the world is both unified and diverse. But diversity is not exclusively, or even principally, cultural. Emphasis on cultural diversity relegates the major differences of position in the economic hierarchy of world capitalism to secondary importance. But it is at the level of the latter that we must begin the attack on the problem. These are manifested not only in inequalities between peoples (culturally different or not, according to circumstance) but also in internal inequalities between classes and social groups. There are no solutions to the crisis except by the reinforcement of the position of the poor and the powerless of the world: the peoples of the peripheries and the dominated social classes of all countries of the centres and peripheries. In other words, escape from global colonialism and liberal myths implies the rejection of neofascist illusions. These principles form the point of departure for meaningful reflection on the construction of a counter-project which is humanist, universalist, democratic, and respectful of diversities, but not inequalities.

I have proposed the construction of a polycentric world as a framework within which negotiated interdependence can be organized in a way which offers dominated peoples and classes improvement in the conditions of their participation in production, and access to better conditions of life. This project implies that we move from action at the level of the nation-state, particularly in the case of small and medium-sized states, to regional political and economic organization, with collective negotiation between regions.

I refer the reader to more detailed arguments I have developed in support of this proposition. We are here concerned with a new conception of regionalization, different from that encapsulated in the present framework of power relations. The latter are constructed like transmission belts of polarizing modernization whereby peripheral zones are attached to dominant centres which share the responsibilities of a 'global colonialism'. NAFTA (North American Free Trade Area attaching Mexico to the United States and Canada), the Lomé Convention (EU-ACP), a yen zone (Japan and South-East Asia), and the proposed Pacific Zone (of the United States, Japan, Australia and the Pacific-rim countries), are neo-imperialist concepts inadequate for the purposes of reducing the development gap. Regional common markets (like Mercosur in Latin America, ECOWAS in West Africa, and the PTA in East and Southern Africa) and political organizations inherited from the Cold War (ASEAN in South-East Asia), have likewise been the object of serious critiques, elaborated elsewhere (*Regionalization in the Third World;* see **Notes** on p. 107).

In contrast to these inadequate visions of regionalization, I have developed arguments in favour of a reconstruction carried out simultaneously at the regional and the global levels, particularly in the area of capital markets and monetary systems. I limit myself here to a summary of some of my conclusions:

(1) It will be necessary to conceive the new World Trade Organization, not as a successor of the GATT, but as an institution charged with planning (dare I use the term?) access to the use of the major natural resources of the globe and the prices of raw materials, without which the environmental discourse remains demagogic rhetoric, manipulated against the interests of humanity as a whole, and the peoples of the periphery in particular. The World Trade Organization should also take responsibility for planning targets for inter-regional trade in industrial products, reconciling general competitiveness, with distributional criteria favouring the disadvantaged regions, and the creation of conditions which permit the improvement of incomes of disadvantaged workers.

(2) It is necessary to put in place mechanisms of organized capital markets to channel excess finance toward productive investment in the peripheries, taking into account the fact that the global market favours financial transfers from the poorest to the richest

countries, and channels excess savings to the United States, enabling it to perpetuate its external payments deficits.

(3) It is necessary to rethink the international monetary system, which has become non-functional, and to replace floating exchange rates and the dollar standard with a system which articulates regional monetary systems (including both the European monetary unit and the regional monies of each of the large regions of the Third World, and that of the ex-USSR) in a way which guarantees relative stability of exchange rates and reinforces the functioning of capital markets as suggested above. I propose this as an alternative to the transformation of the IMF into a world central bank, on the grounds that this is utopian and dangerous, given the polarizing tendencies of global capital markets.

The functions and purposes of the regions which are suggested are not limited to spaces of preferential economic integration. They should serve equally as political spaces favouring the collective reinforcement of the social position of disadvantaged classes and sub-regions. This regionalization is not intended to be confined to the continents of the Third World but also to serve the European spaces.

The perspective of such a compromise between globalization and local and regional autonomy (which I have called a 'coherent delinking' in response to the new challenges) would demand a serious revision of the concept of 'development assistance', and the democratization of the UN system, which could then be employed to implement the objectives of disarmament (facilitated by measures of regional and national security within the framework of regional reconstruction). The UN would be able to put in place a system of world taxation (closely related to the management of the world's natural resources), and complement its own organization as a system of inter-state relations with a world parliament able to reconcile the requirements of universalism (individual rights, collective rights of peoples, political and social rights) with the diversity of our historic and cultural heritage.

It is well understood that the totality of this project has no chance of realization unless social forces able to carry out the necessary reforms crystallize first at the level of the nation-state, because there is no possibility of reform within the structures imposed by global liberalization and polarization. Reform at the sectoral level (reorganization of administration, taxation, education, support for participatory development) and a more general vision of the democratization of societies and their political and economic management are preliminary steps and stages which cannot be short-circuited or circumvented. Without them the vision of a reorganized planetary order able to save the world from chaos and crisis and re-launch development remains fatally and perfectly utopian.

Notes

In order to avoid unnecessary repetition, the above text has summarized the conclusions of reflections developed more fully elsewhere:

The nature of the postwar 'cycle':
S. Amin (ed.) *Mondialisation et Accumulation* (L'Harmattan, 1994): pp. 10–19 (the 'three pillars' which constitute the base of postwar expansion and the reasons for their erosion); S. Amin, *Re-Reading the Post-War Period: An Intellectual Itinerary* (Monthly Review Press, 1994), Chapter 8 (collapse of the mechanisms of capitalist regulation)

New forms of the exploitation and forms of global polarization (with emphasis on what I have called the 'five monopolies' which reproduce polarization in the new conditions and corresponding forms of the globalized law of value)

S. Amin, 'The Future of Global Polarization' (University of Nagoya, 1994): Chapter 1 in *Review*, Binghampton, New York

Political management of the crisis:
S. Amin, *Empire of Chaos* (Monthly Review Press, 1993): Chapter 1 ('Empire of Chaos', Chapter 2 ('The New Capitalist Globalization'), Chapter 5 ('Regional Conflicts'); and 'Les stratégies militaires de l'hégémonie américaine' in S. Amin (ed.) *Les enjeux stratégiques en Méditerranée* (L'Harmattan, 1992): pp. 11–105; S. Amin, *The* 'Rise of Ethnicity' (Chapter 4 in this volume)

Critiques of the Bretton Woods order, and arguments in favour of proposed reforms: see Chapters 2 and 3 in this volume, and S. Amin, *Regionalization in the Third World in Response to the Challenge of Polarizing Globalization* (WIDER, forthcoming)

References
Casanova, P. G. (ed.), *Etat et Politique dans le Tiers Monde*, L'Harmattan, Paris, 1994
Polyanyi, Karl, *The Great Transformation*, London, 1944

CHAPTER 6

The Challenges Posed by Globalization: The European Case

The period after the Second World War was a good one for Western Europe. In the space of a few decades, the countries of the region recovered the ground lost since 1913 and caught up with the United States, which had until then been the only country to benefit from the two wars. Even ancestral national hatreds seemed bound to disappear as a new generation and a new sense of Europeanness took hold. In this context, the gradual construction of the European Economic Community (EEC) really does seem to have served some useful functions; its balance-sheet is indisputably positive. But then the crisis broke: high growth-rates without precedent in history tailed off; steadily rising standards of living no longer appeared credible; and unemployment, after dropping out of the picture for thirty years, made a sudden, massive and long-term re-entry. At present, a European Union fascinated by its own success is hastening to expand eastward. Will it be able to meet the new challenges facing it? And if so, on what conditions?

The Lack of Political Complementarity in the Postwar European Economic Community Project

1. In the aftermath of the Second World War, all the peoples of Europe were confronted with huge challenges that fuelled all kinds of fears, both well-founded and illusory.

Europe was divided in two. But although, in the shared imagination, each half seemed to threaten the other, there was absolutely no risk of military aggression.

The postwar period was bound to be a time of peace – a peace which was not, as too often suggested, due only to the American nuclear umbrella and the superpower balance of terror. In fact, military balance was achieved very late in the day – around the year 1970 – when reconstruction had been completed for nearly twenty years and the ensuing European miracle was beginning to run out of steam (not that this attracted much attention). By that time, some even thought of American military protection as improper.

If the Soviet regime had had the aim of invading Western Europe, it would have shown it much sooner. In reality, it never abandoned the defensive posture of an encircled country which it first adopted after 1917. Stalin, who was certainly not a great socialist democrat but was not mad as was Hitler, wanted no more than a protective buffer, although this was, it is true, conceived in the outmoded terms of a military strategy.

The United States, for its part, thought of an eventual rollback only as a gradual process; it too was alive to the dangers of attacking militarily. The vision of world hegemony in which America is still steeped did not derive from Hitler's mad and criminal methods! There was thus no reason to be surprised when the Soviet Union held back from supporting the Greek Communists between 1945 and 1947, or when Washington refrained from intervening in Hungary in 1956. The only countries to liberate themselves from Moscow's tutelage – Yugoslavia in 1948, Albania from 1960 on – did so without support or even exuberant sympathy from the West.

But if there was no risk of war, was there not perhaps a danger of revolutions? That was what people thought in the two camps into which opinion was divided, at least in France and Italy, although history would show it to be a twofold illusion. Of course, if reconstruction had marked time instead of taking off as it did, no one can say how the peoples of Europe would have reacted. After all, they were still full of the anti-fascist spirit and had only scornful memories of the inter-war regimes, so would they not perhaps have been won over by what was presented as the victorious beginnings of socialist construction in the East? I have my doubts. And even if they had moved in that direction, I doubt whether the local conservative forces and the American armies would have accepted a *fait accompli*. (We know from their secret agreement that these forces did not accept it, and planned to answer a Communist victory, even an electoral victory, with a *coup d'état*.) Moscow would have been thoroughly embarrassed by such a present, which would have threatened to challenge its own conceptions of socialism. Anyway, I do not think that all these rather fanciful hypotheses deserve more of our attention. There were no reasons why reconstruction should not speed ahead, and the United States, being aware of the challenge, helped out with the Marshall Plan.

Another thing worrying public opinion throughout Europe after the war – one whose importance we tend to forget today – was the fear of a revival of Germany's industrial and military power. Stalin wanted his buffer zone so that he could face up to it. Britain opted for a perpetual and unconditional alliance in the tow of the United States. France, whose position as a great power was now a thing of the past, was particularly sensitive to the potential threat from Germany. How was it to be circumvented? There was a fleeting idea of simply dismantling Germany, but that was soon abandoned. De Gaulle, who had knuckled under as a subaltern ally, kept mixed feelings with regard to the American protector. On the other hand, an alliance with Moscow threatened to strengthen the position of the Communists. The new idea that then forced its way in was to neutralize Germany by absorbing it into the goal of building Europe. This idea met the concern to root democracy east of the Rhine, as well as the concern to open markets in a way required for the unfurling of American hegemony. In order to end the strongly protectionist, if not actually autarkic, tendencies of interwar Europe, the Marshall Plan thus aimed to support the intensification of intra-European trade as a prelude to a complete opening up. This was the exact opposite of the choice made half a century later *vis-à-vis* Eastern Europe, where the Western powers and the organizations inspired by them immediately intervened to dismantle the mutual dependences established within Comecon (whose official name was, of course, the Council for Mutual Economic Aid) – even though this negatively affected reconstruction in the East.

The project of a European Community was born in the postwar atmosphere just described. It has been necessary to recall it so as to understand the way in which things developed later.

2. At the level of historical detail, we know that the European project found its first expression in the creation of the Coal and Steel Community (ECSC) in 1951, which was Jean Monnet's response to French fears of a revival of Germany's military-industrial complex: industry across the Rhine would instead be absorbed into the construction of Europe. On the other hand, a parallel project to neutralize the Bundeswehr by integrating it into a European army (under the umbrella of a European Defence Community) was scuppered in 1954. The reconstituted German army has, it is true, been restricted in three ways: (i) by the Federal Republic's participation in NATO; (ii) by its lack of nuclear weapons; and (iii) by constitutional provisions (now under heavy attack) that limit any intervention outside its frontiers. Nevertheless, the German military question has remained a source of concern, and no doubt this was what led de Gaulle to sabotage Euratom

(founded in 1957) in favour of the (French) Atomic Energy Commission and membership of the nuclear club.

Historical details do sometimes make grand history. The success of the ECSC was only provisional (as steel and coal lost their function as engines of the economy). But this success, together with the failure of the political dimension (in the Defence Community project) and the coming to power of de Gaulle, shifted the main axis of European construction towards economic integration on the basis of the 1957 Treaty of Rome, while the whole question of political power, though not totally forgotten, fell a long way behind.

This imbalance is today at the heart of the challenge facing Europe. Can it be corrected by speeding up the construction of political Europe? Is that what people want? Is it desirable? Is it otherwise possible to consolidate the economic gains? We shall come back to all these questions.

The building of 'economic Europe' implied a series of choices whose long-term range made them decisive. Was the aim solely to create a stronger free-trade zone open to a world system that should itself be opened up as much as possible? Or was the idea to develop a structure (not necessarily as extreme as 'fortress Europe') that could resist outside influences considered to be negative? In other words, should Europe complement or compete with America and Japan? The choice, latent at each stage and in each great decision, has not in my view been clearly made. Nor can it be, given the differences of opinion not only between member-states but also within the public opinion of the various countries.

The political aspect, still taking its first faltering steps, cannot seriously influence the decisions affecting economic integration. And yet, the economic choices presuppose, at least implicitly, political options that are consistent with them. The conflict is clearly between the conception of a politically integrated Europe (with a supranational government, however called) and the vision of a merely coordinated 'Europe of Nations' (to use the Gaullist formula that is also the constant position of Britain). Here too the question is: to do what? Is the perspective still that of a North Atlantic grouping running in tandem with NATO? Or is it that of an independent rival which, without necessarily saying its name, might point towards a European neo-imperialism?

In withholding or delaying a decision at this political level, Europe actually chose to move ahead only with the building of a common market (potentially, but not yet, a single market). It was a choice that followed the line of least resistance, of the lowest common denominator. And, as I said before, its longer-term significance made it a right-wing option.

I do not mean that it was the choice of the European (conservative and liberal) Right as opposed to the (socialist) Left. For attachment to the European project, or reservations about it, cut across party lines. Total or near-total rejection (though threatening to spread) is today the position of a fairly small minority. Things were not always so. Doubts carried the day for a long time in some countries that have only recently joined (the Scandinavias). The European idea is alien to the fascists of the far Right, even if they do not say so openly. The Communist parties were opposed in principle to the 'Europe of traders', but then joined it without being in a position to negotiate the terms. The Right as a whole has always grouped together divergent economic interests. Segments of modern and competitive big capital (in industry, agri-business or finance) nearly always prefer open markets, while other sectors of industry – often the ones in decline – evidently need to cling to whatever national protection is available. The Right has thus always contained many different shades, or even divisions, according to the concrete issues under discussion in Brussels. The same is true of the Left. Even if one assumes that it is less sensitive to various employers' interests (which is not necessarily the case), it is sensitive to the no-less divergent workers' interests. Will the concrete forms of market expansion operate in favour of upward homogenization, through a kind of 'trickle-down effect' promoting wage increases and greater social benefits for deprived layers? Or will they, on the contrary, weigh in favour of downward homogenization by sharpening competition between workers, especially in a period of crisis? Opinions are still divided on these questions, and of course they vary according to the field of action and the type of decision involved. Moreover, ideological perceptions are never absent, either on the Right (where nationalism is common enough but hostility to communism has also been running at maximum intensity) or on the Left (where internationalist perspectives are theoretically more congenial but nationalism is not absent either).

The point I am making, then, is that advance along the line of least resistance allowed the opening of markets to take off, while in the realm of social and political management Europe was always nervous about touching the national structures already in place. But the mere opening of markets naturally strengthened capital and improved its position in the antagonistic relationship with labour. A balance could have been maintained only if social measures had simultaneously framed the market, at least reproducing at an enlarged (European) level the conditions under which the capital/labour relation functioned at the previous level of narrower (national) markets.

The EC's Achievements: A Balance-Sheet

1. As far as economic (and even social) development is concerned, the balance-sheet of the EC is nevertheless indisputably positive. The real question is to know why this is so. A dogmatic neoliberal economist would quite simply say that the opening of markets stimulated growth, which had a trickle-down effect on the whole of the population, workers and businessmen alike. In my view, this thesis is wrong as to both the causal relationship between market and expansion, and the effects on the distribution of income. On the one hand, it was expansion that opened the markets, not *vice versa*: on the other hand, the trickle-down effects mostly exist in the neoliberal imagination, or are the fruit of social conquests won against the one-sided logic of the market.

The positive balance-sheet is therefore due to something quite different. The real engine of growth in postwar Europe was the social compromise between capital and labour, which resulted from the victory over fascism and an ensuing balance of forces more favourable to the workers than at any previous time in the history of capitalism. The welfare state, built throughout Western Europe on the solid basis of what some have called 'Fordism', paved the way for the exceptional growth of the postwar years. In this context, of course, the opening of markets was not only possible and straightforward; it was also a way of boosting the potential of the model to expand. If, as the textbooks claim, the opening of markets had taken place without the internal dynamism of the welfare state, the outcome would almost certainly have been the opposite: a worsening of production results, such as we see today in the African, Arab and Latin American Third World. But the welfare state in question was national, in the sense that it functioned through strictly national state policies in support of a characteristic 'social contract' between capital and labour (the essence of this contract being to ensure that wages rose in parallel with productivity at national level).

The effectiveness of these national policies is also the reason why the opening of markets did not increase but actually reduced the inequalities benefiting the most dynamic countries. The clearest example of this is Italy, which climbed up the European ladder by virtue of its exceptionally high growth-rates. Was the EC to thank for this? The EC did contribute to it, for sure: not only by opening the huge European market to the industry of northern Italy, but also by supporting the modernization drive in the South. This contribution was of secondary importance, however, in comparison with the internal distribution carried out by the Italian state. Spain, before joining the EC, also recorded growth-rates that were leading it to catch up. Thus, the decisive factor in the success attributed to the EC was, in fact, national policies built around Fordism and the welfare state (of however poor a kind). In the absence of organized social counterweights, with powerful state policies to support them, the opening of markets always has a polarizing rather than an inequality-reducing effect.

2. Apart from the exceptional growth of the three decades from 1950 to 1980, the EC has a number of other striking achievements to its credit. The main one of these, in my view, is the Common Agricultural Policy (CAP), which has delinked agricultural prices by setting intervention prices higher than those on the so-called world market. This assures farmers an income comparable to those of the urban world, as well as protection in the form of levies that raise the prices of agricultural imports to Community levels. In this way, the EC gave a huge boost to its agriculture, so that Europe has not only become self-sufficient but is itself a major exporter. This success is now something of a problem, however, because unuseable surpluses have been piling up in spite of the support given to exporters through the payment of sums equivalent to the levies. With the successes gained, the EC is in a position, if necessary, gradually to lower its intervention prices. It is deplorable that Europe, having implemented in this area the fundamental principle of delinking, should be denying to Third World countries the right to do the same!

The European Monetary System, designed to protect the EC from the wild dollar fluctuations of 1972 and after, was beginning to show favourable results by the end of the 1970s. The absurd monetarist dogmas currently in fashion have obscured the real reason for this success, which needs to be made the object of serious discussion. Was it due to the underlying principle of the system, or rather to a conjuncture that led the principal member-states to run their general (not just monetary) economic policies along parallel lines? I myself incline towards the latter explanation and would therefore conclude that the system remains rather shaky – as the successive crises since 1992 should have shown. In this area, unlike in agriculture, Europe has not opted for delinking. Global liberalization of capital movements – the principle that Europe embraced after the United States had done so – has combined with the end of growth to reduce the effectiveness of the collective protection of European currencies, and by ricocheting their collective solidarity. Sooner or later, this fragility will almost inevitably force the member-states to adopt divergent economic and monetary policies. And in my view, the only protection against this development – which would considerably reduce the extent of the 'broad market' and the prospects of economic integration – is here again to delink: that is, to acquire at Community level (or, failing that, at national level) the means of regulating capital transfers so as to reduce the devastating effects of financial speculation.

Before and immediately after the Second World War, the gaps in development and living standards between Mediterranean Europe (Italy and Spain) and Northern Europe (with France in the middle and Britain facing historic decline) were still immense. Since then there has been a remarkable narrowing of these gaps, and it has to be asked whether this can be attributed to the building of the European Community. I am arguing that these successes should be credited as much to the effective national policies of France, Italy and Spain in particular, as to the opportunities offered by market expansion. As far as EC subsidies to deprived countries and regions are concerned, market expansion played no more than a supporting role. As we know, Ireland, Portugal, Greece, Southern Italy and the former East Germany do receive quite significant subsidies. But at least in the last two regions, the success or failure of their economic reconstruction will depend more upon the political strategies and action of the respective states. Nor is it certain, in the case of Greece, that such subsidies have had a positive effect; it is possible that they have helped to drive the country up a blind alley – perhaps because it joined the EC before it was sufficiently competitive, and so is now marginalized in subaltern functions such as tourism. This problem, which has to do more generally with the devastating effects of peripheral capitalist integration into world markets, may tomorrow be the one facing countries of Eastern Europe pressed to join the EC. One often hears it said that it is better to integrate into, rather than remain outside, the groupings formed around developed poles – or, more naïvely expressed, that it is always possible to take advantage of dependence on a developed centre. But this is an illusion kept alive by the dominant ideology, which has been cruelly refuted by history. Does not Haiti depend upon the United States, for example? There may sometimes be pull-along effects, but there are also devastation effects which the dogmatic opponents of delinking wish to ignore on principle.

If one looks more closely at what happened in Europe during the great boom of 1950 to 1980, it becomes clear that while inequality between countries more or less declined, regional inequalities within countries often intensified. The EC is certainly not responsible for such trends: they are a natural product of capitalist expansion whose effects could have been combated only through bolder national policies.

Despite the achievements on the credit side of the EC, the single market is not yet a fully-fledged reality. Energy and transport still largely fall outside the Community structures, belonging instead to national, and therefore partly conflictual, dynamics. Yet the Community has set out on the path of integrating them into the single market, by means of the deregulation and privatization currently under way. These options are negative, in my view, because the sectors involved are oligopolistic (or even monopolistic) by their very nature – which is why so many of them were nationalized. The new measures are thus substituting private oligopolies for public monopolies, with no guarantee that the characteristic logic of the private sector will yield results consistent with the demand for optimal development of the European area as a whole. Indeed, it is to be feared that the logic of short-term profit will in these cases accentuate inequalities of development. The alternative would have been planned coordination by the community of states. But the dominant ideological prejudices, and the subordination of governments to the quest of finance capital for lucrative investment, have been responsible for most unfortunate choices in this domain.

More serious still, in my eyes, is the fact that the EC has not developed its own industrial policies. The member-states have sometimes done so, but they themselves tend to tune in with the liberal, anti-state music of the times. As to research and development, which everyone today regards as crucially important, Europe continues to lag behind the United States and Japan; and Community projects to alleviate the effects of national inadequacies remain extremely limited in scope.

Despite the generally positive balance-sheet of the EC, therefore, Europe has not really taken a road that would allow it to move beyond a free-trade zone (a pseudo single market) to achieve genuine economic integration. Such integration would require that a European productive system gradually replaced the national productive systems inherited from the past. But the qualitative leap implied by such an advance would require the solution of political problems that have scarcely yet been posed.

In these conditions, it would be wrong to attach to the growth of intra-Community trade the importance that it has in triumphalist discourses. It is true that such trade rose from a figure between 25 per cent and 40 per cent for various member-states around 1960 (little different from the eve of the First or Second World Wars) to reach current levels of 50 to 60 per cent. But this advance, which certainly testifies to the new solidity of EC preferences, is not the same as an integrated productive system.

3. Finally, our critical presentation of the Community's economic achievements should look at the budget, which summarizes well their nature, scope and limitations.

The EC budget, though not trifling, is still limited to a mere 2.4 per cent of the total budgets of member-states. Its funds come from customs duties (28 per cent), as in any customs union, from levies on agricultural imports (3 per cent) which have declined through the very success of the CAP, from levies on VAT (51 per cent), and from contributions of member-states proportionate to their GNP (27 per cent). The concern to assure so-called normal competitive conditions is, of course, at the root of the tax harmonization being pursued by the EC. In accordance with the orthodox financial doctrine that only indirect taxes enter into the formation of prices, it has been agreed that VAT – by far the most important for price formation – should be roughly harmonized through the adoption of a lower limit of 25 per cent (although the actual rates will vary between 15 per cent and 25 per cent from country to country). Again in accordance with conventional doctrine, it has not been thought necessary that income tax should be harmonized. My own opinion is that this doctrine is not very solid, and that it stands in need of considerable qualification. For the structure of income distribution (which is affected by income tax) is one of the factors determining relative prices, and therefore influences the conditions of competition. Strong economic integration will demand harmonization of income tax, but public opinion is a long way from accepting this in the various countries of Europe.

As to expenditure, the EC budget is allocated to CAP support (50 per cent), regional aid (30 per cent), aid to the Third World (5 per cent) and research and development) (4 per cent). Because of the CAP's success and the difficulties in exporting Europe's output surplus, the share of support assigned to agricultural exports has been tending to decline, down from 80 per cent just a few years ago to 50 per cent today. Support for deprived regions, on the other hand, has shot up as a result of German unification. Public opinion in many European countries sometimes finds it hard to accept that Germany should not bear the full cost of this eminently political decision, which anyway strengthens its position as the major power within the EC. By contrast, assistance to Third World countries cuts a pretty sorry figure (a sixth of the aid given to peripheral European regions, for a population ten to twenty times more numerous!). Such sums make it look more like charity than international solidarity, and at any event it has not reached the minimum level at which it could be an instrument for building a Euro-African regional area. This fact expresses something that is not always grasped: namely, that in spite of association agreements between the EC and the ACP (Africa, Caribbean Pacific Group), there is no political vision of relations between Europe, on the one hand, and the Arab world, sub-

Saharan Africa and the Third World in general, on the other. It is not even certain that the member-states – or some of them – have any concept of such relations or of the world-scale regionalization issues that they imply.

The Future of European Integration in the Age of Globalization

1. The balance-sheet of the EC's achievements has clearly brought out the main feature of the construction of Europe. So far, this has been almost entirely limited to the creation of an open trading area – not yet even an economic area on the road to integration. So far, the absence of a political concept of Europe has stymied any attempt to go further. All Europeans are perfectly aware of this fact, and most of them deplore it. Instruments of political construction have, as we shall see, been created, but we are a long way from knowing what purpose they are meant to serve. Meanwhile the lack of political vision, and its inevitable complement at the level of social perspectives, is reacting upon the Community's already-established economic infrastructure. It remains an open question how Europe and the states constituting it intend to locate their project (or projects) within the world economic and political system.

The future of European integration is therefore still quite unsettled. Integration might grow deeper until Europe becomes a new political and social subject, but the Community might equally well stagnate, become marginal, even go into reverse and lose the significance it has so far acquired. Europe has not made itself an irreversible historical reality.

Whenever the European project threatened to challenge what was considered a key element of national sovereignty, it gave the impression of reaching the limits of the possible. And the frontier was not crossed. Let me give a few examples from a doubtless long list.

(1) Research and development (R&D) is essentially a national responsibility, which is transferred to agencies of the Community only in a very limited number of non-vital areas. Is one reason for this not the fact that R&D is closely bound up with the development of military capacity, as the example of Euratom should remind us?

(2) Public markets are not presently subject to genuine, Community-wide competition. By various, sometimes roundabout means, the member-states ensure that transparency does not challenge the

national preference which, in this case, they associate with the exercise of sovereignty.

(3) Commercial law, especially company law, remains the business of the national states. Projects to unify it – which are an almost self-evident requirement for the emergence of 'European' (and not just German, British or French) multinationals – do not get beyond the level of rhetorical speeches and academic studies.

(4) Cinema and TV productions have been excluded from the sphere subject to commercial competition, on the grounds of 'making an exception for culture'. France, more sensitive than others to the threat of an American cultural invasion, has placed itself in the van of this struggle and – quite rightly, in my view – invoked the close relationship between cultural independence and straightforward political independence.

As the Community is not a state or even the embryo of one, it immediately steps aside from any problem of sovereignty and leaves the individual states to join (or decline) battle, whether in serried or scattered ranks.

Yet the problems concerning the future of the Community – will it develop the credentials of a multinational or supranational state? – are all the more difficult to identify in as much as the relationship between state and economic integration has itself been overturned by recent trends in the world (and not just in Europe).

So far, there has never been real economic integration except in the area defined by national sovereignty. The history of the formation of modern (bourgeois) nation-states involved the simultaneous construction of an integrated, autocentred economic area – that is, of a national productive system and a national political system (sometimes, of course, embracing more than one actual nation). This concordance provided the model which countries arriving later in modernity or independence attempted to reproduce. The apparent exceptions confirm the rule. The colonial empires were hierarchical spaces organized around the autocentred metropolis. And if today the USA and Canada form an almost perfectly integrated area, this is due to the imbalance between these two powers, Canada having agreed in effect to be an external province of the United States. Regional hegemonies (such as that of the US in Latin America or of Europe in Africa), or world hegemonies (such as that of Britain in the nineteenth century or of the United States after 1945), do not operate within an integrated economic space – far from it. They organize the hierarchy of the regions making up the system.

It is sometimes claimed that, since this concordance between state and integrated economic area is in the course of disappearing, we will in future see integrated economic areas which do not coincide with a single state, or which comprise a constellation of states around a power whose leadership, not to say hegemony, they accept. Europe would be the example of such a tendency: it will integrate as an economic entity (or at least that is desirable and feasible), but no Community-state will be formed, nor will there be acceptance of the leadership of one of its member-states (which could only be Germany). An alternative view would be that the concordance between state and integrated economic area will continue to assert itself, so that Europe will either build its own Community-state, or accept the 'German Europe' formula, or break apart.

These two schools of thought accept that globalization is leading inevitably to the break-up of national productive systems, that the construction of a global productive system is both necessary and inescapable (with regional sub-areas as a first stage and then a constituent part), and that this desirable evolution will need to be managed politically and socially. To oppose it is to spurn progress and cling to a bygone past, with all the generally dramatic consequences that such a non-starter of a strategy implies. To reject a 'German Europe' at the same time would be in effect to accept that globalization should continue in a diffuse manner under American hegemony. The image of such a world is of a system of fragmented and impotent powers (one could hardly dare call them states) subject to the exigencies of an all-pervasive market – or, in other words, to the particular logic of the 'multinationals', the tough segments of a globalized productive system. The gendarme of this world 'order' could only be the United States, the sole military power and the only state in the full sense of the word, even if that military power and that state agreed to operate under the flag of a loose world political organization (the UN). For some, this prospect is perfectly acceptable, even a desirable advance in economic globalization and a contribution to the democratization of society. For others, it is nothing of the kind. For me, it is anyway an unattainable utopia.

So, we are left with the stubborn question of the future of Europe. What should be our starting-point? I would say that it should be 'actually existing' Europe, which has the following characteristics:

(1) It is not an integrated economic area, but only approximates to a large preferential market; there is no European productive system, there are no European productive entities, no European

multinationals. In these conditions, the undoubted erosion of national productive systems does not promote a recomposition of European productive systems, but proceeds by tearing bits away and linking them up with globalized productive systems. The British option is, in this sense, highly illuminating. The City – the most glittering remnant of the past which, now part of the globalized finance system, allows Britain to keep going in the teeth of decline – gives its preference to the demands of globalization rather than to the construction of a financial Europe. British industry has been following suit, as the implantation of the Japanese motor industry makes clear. But it would be wrong to think that Britain is the exception; real behaviour in German, French or Italian industry is no different.

(2)   As things stand, Europe is not based on any common project for the shaping of society. To convince oneself of the truth of this harsh judgement, one has only to look at the minor role of the 'social dimension' in Community regulations. I do not underestimate certain principles that now form part of majority opinion in all (or nearly all) European societies and as such are endorsed by the Community itself. Equal treatment for men and women is one of these new conquests, as is the general principle of ecological protection. But otherwise the Community's common denominator does not cover very much; after all, controlled working conditions or trade union rights were achieved long ago in the principal member-states. Neither the key question of social ownership (going beyond the limited debate over private versus public ownership), nor the future of work and its place in society (apart from a few banalities about 'consultation' of workers) is on the agenda for action by the Community. It is true that they are not up for decision in the member-states either. For now that the national welfare state (the great project for half a century) has exhausted its potential, Europe no longer has a vision of society with which to move ahead. This lack is due not only to the grip of the traditional Right over current affairs – for in the past that Right was compelled to manage the welfare state in alternation with the Left of the time; today, the lack affects the European Left just as much. The common denominator of democratic practice in the management of political life does not by itself compensate for this lack. And if it is thought to be enough, it threatens to crumble in turn.

(3) Europe is not an entity with a common vision – or, to be even harsher, any vision at all – of its relationship to other regions of the planet. This is felt not only in the sphere of economics; as I said before, Europeans (states, parties, public opinion) have not made a choice between integration in the process of globalization and truly preferential community integration (which would imply a dose of delinking, to use an unpopular term). The lack of vision concerns also the political side of things. Do Europeans want to bring in Eastern Europe and the ex-USSR? Or do they want to 'Latin Americanize' them? Do they conceive of leaving behind the colonial or quasi-colonial tradition in their relations with Africa and the Arab world? And as to the 'development' of Asia – about whose meaning, scale and quality I have grave doubts – do Europeans have any feelings other than those inspired by fear? How many times will we hear it repeated that the all-European trade deficit with all the countries of Asia (Japan, China and the 'Tigers') is unacceptable – whereas reverse imbalances with other regions are perfectly acceptable! Europe's lack of anything other than run-of-the-mill ideas connected to the management of petty interests does have one major consequence. It leaves the United States with a 'world-view' monopoly and the (military) means to try to administer it.

2. All these weaknesses are by no means lost on the Europeans, who have even provided themselves with some means of preparing the ground for the future. But as we shall see, the answers they seem to want to give to the challenge are inadequate.

The average European citizen knows perfectly well what the local council or the national parliament or government represents for him. But he is completely at sea in the realm of EC institutions. It is by analysing what these are and do, however, that some headway can be made in the debate concerning the nature of the changes and how they are to be met.

The Commission is not, as some have argued, a disparate bunch of services run by technocrats. Nor is it a (supranational) government – since the commissioners are responsible not for one field in a ministerial type of division of labour (for example, agriculture, industry, finance), but for special tasks delegated to the Community. The Commission is not even the embryo of a government, since none of the responsibilities involving the exercise of sovereignty has been entrusted to it (for example, police, army, foreign affairs, justice). We know how dangerous this shortfall threatens to become: 'Europol', for instance, would lack any transparency and involve no more than collaboration between national police forces far from the gaze of public scrutiny. This is also why the president of the Commission is not a prime minister responsible for general policy and coordination of the activity of ministers placed under him.

The tasks of defining policy and delegating or organizing executive powers are therefore fulfilled, outside the Commission, by the Council. We ought rather to say Councils, as they are meetings of ministers of the states concerned. The inconsistencies of this type of organization have often been pointed out: the finance ministers, for example, may take a decision that conflicts with one already reached by agriculture ministers. At national level, such clashes are avoided through the existence of a Council of Ministers and a prime minister – but here these do not exist.

Is the European Parliament such a body? Or is it at least the embryo of a genuine European Assembly? Nothing has been decided in this domain. Approval of the budget (virtually predetermined by the decisions of the Council) and the choice of commissioners remain formal acts devoid of responsibility. Moreover, the idea that Euro MPs should be elected on transnational lists by the whole European electorate does not seem to have ripened in the political and cultural thinking of the continent.

Community institutions, in the end, have the status of policy-implementation services acting on behalf of an inter-state government that does not speak its name. The latter cannot adopt a clear strategic viewpoint on basic problems, if only because European governments change with national parliamentary majorities and these majorities, whether Left or Right, are not the same as those expressed at a European level. More important still, however, is the fact that no dominant vision can be identified within each of the member-states. There is no 'German' or 'French' or 'British' concept of the future of European integration, even if at any given moment each national government has a position on the questions of the hour. We cannot even say that the Right and the Left have general contrasting visions of Europe. Quite different, sometimes totally divergent, points of view are to be found within both political camps in each country. Opinions on this issue are thus a real puzzle for the European analyst and politician. But this is neither an advantage nor a drawback at the present stage, because European institutions have only very clearly defined executive responsibilities.

3. Europe is today facing the new challenges of both the crisis and its own eastward expansion.

The opening of the market, conceived as virtually the only axis of

Europe-building, did not pose serious problems when economic growth proceeded smoothly on the basis of the welfare state, and when the EC was limited to a Western Europe composed mainly of countries quite close in terms of development. Any difficulties that arose were always minor and sectoral, and they could be overcome without great sacrifice. The same cannot be said, however, of present-day conditions. Mass unemployment is probably here to stay unless the basic concepts of social labour change in a radical direction. And together with major unevenness of development within a Community extended (however gradually) to the whole continent, this poses a challenge in the face of which open markets are an ineffective, and more than dubious, magic formula.

Europe is actually confronted with three types of problem requiring decisions which, without a doubt, are objectively difficult:

(1) The choice of a final vision of European political integration cannot be postponed or evaded indefinitely. Without simplifying too much, we could define this choice as follows. Is the idea to end up with a supranational political power (usually called the 'federalist' option in Eurojargon)? Or is the goal only a 'Europe of nations' (sometimes known in the jargon as the 'confederal' solution) – that is, a Europe composed of states that remain the only sovereign powers at the political level? Supporters of the latter solution think it is compatible with economic integration that will complete and strengthen the single market. My own view, expressed earlier, is that it is of doubtful realism, in that advanced economic integration is impossible without the construction of a common political power. Otherwise, the economic aspect of the project will progress only with great difficulty beyond the single market, and gains in this area will themselves remain fragile and reversible.

At any event, even on the most 'Europeanist' hypothesis, it would be futile, illusory and dangerous to ignore the solid attachments to strong national realities constructed by history. It will therefore be necessary to use great imagination in devising institutional forms capable of reconciling such attachments with a common Europeanness that may develop. The historical experience of Europe or other parts of the world provides no model, federal nor confederal, in answer to this new and specific challenge.

Whatever the option, it would still probably be the case that **multi-track integration cannot be avoided**. This is obvious enough in the federalist hypothesis. But even in the confederal one, which does not seek to limit national political sovereignties, the same single economic system cannot be imposed on all European societies, especially if the Community expands to the east, and still less can it be imposed rapidly, unless that system is defined exclusively by the lowest common denominator of a large open market. Various speeds of advance will therefore be inevitable at any event. This said, let me repeat what I argued earlier: any attempt to move beyond the common market towards economic integration of only a 'hard core' of the European Community, without a common political power, is doomed to failure.

(2)   The European continent, which is probably cut out (by virtue of its Europeanness?) to form a regional entity in tomorrow's world, is far from being homogeneous. It is not only that it consists of nations whose reality could not be erased (and many think that planing-down universalization of this kind is not even desirable). There is also the fact that the structures and development levels of its constituent parts are different and uneven.

It is not hard to trace the frontiers of the core regions; although they belong to different countries, they have strong characteristics in common and comparable levels of development. But moving out towards the four cardinal points – to the south-west, north-west, south-east and east – the challenges facing societies today, and certainly for a long time to come, are of different natures.

To be effective, even a purely economic project to encompass the core and its peripheries cannot be based upon ignorance of the problems posed by such heterogenity. A common market, and only that, is not necessarily desirable for all. The example of Greece has been mentioned already, and unless appropriate protective fencing is systematically put in place, the membership of East European countries might aggravate the distortions caused by the functioning of market laws.

(3)   The most disturbing thing, in my opinion, is not that Europeans have failed to raise these problems (they have identified them quite precisely), but that the first steps to a solution seem to be driving the project up a blind alley.

As we know, the Maastricht Treaty that instituted the new

'European Union' drained off the main political challenge facing Europe. Having evaded the difficulty, it shunted the construction of Europe not into a siding but into what I see as a real dead-end. The treaty gave priority to the creation of a single currency (the Euro): in other words, it decided to pursue the project of economic integration by taking a crucial step (single currency) in the absence of political perspectives for the Union.

The reasoning behind this choice is well known: if a single market, freedom of capital movements and stability of exchange rates are to be guaranteed simultaneously, a common monetary policy (and ultimately a single currency) is a necessary condition. I believe that this reasoning is flawed at two levels:

(a)   The three objectives can be reconciled with one another only if, beyond a common monetary policy, the economic and social policies of the member-states also run in parallel. What I mean by this is that, if the system is to function, the policies of member-states (for example, taxation, public expenditure) must be identical, the strategies of sectors and branches of the productive system must run along similar lines, the strategies of the social actors (especially the trade unions) must also be on the same course, and so on.

(b)   It is difficult – and impossible in times of crisis – to formulate a coherent and effective European policy that will at once guarantee 'internal opening' and 'external opening' (of markets and capital flows). A choice must be made. To make internal opening the priority means that protective fencing is required. But as we have seen, any talk of delinking has been placed under a cloud.

This unfortunate turn is, in my view, due to the fashionable dominance of monetarist ideology, and to nothing else. It is suggested that any social entity (member-state or Community) can practise 'neutral monetary management'. My own view is that this is a purely ideological concept which has no real or lasting historical existence. Neutral management exists in appearance only at moments when society, lacking an overall project, bows to the one-sided law of the market. But history shows that such moments are actually chaotic transitions towards a new social order, defined by a project for society as a whole. The currency then becomes what it is by nature: not a commodity like any other (as fashionable neoliberal ideology claims), but an operational instrument of the collective will.

Europe, then, has gone for a miracle cure, hoping to rid itself of the difficult political choices with which it is confronted. However, the pursuit of a neutral monetary policy by the Bundesbank, and by other central banks behind it, is not destined to become a long-term feature of the situation. It will last as long as the conservative forces in charge insist on managing the crisis in the way they do: that is, at the cost of a descending spiral that continually widens the scale of the crisis. We can bet that the social storms produced by this policy – which are already becoming visible – will put an end to it sooner than expected. Already the 1996 target-date for creation of the Euro has been shifted forward to 1999. Soon it will be postponed to the Greek calends.

4. Reeling from the priority given to a common currency, the building of Europe has entered a stormy zone. This priority strengthens the most conservative forces which are attached to a way of managing the crisis without end. The clamour of protests against its inevitable consequences will undoubtedly grow louder still. For the tying of the European project to an extreme neoliberal policy may reverse general attitudes in the very near future, and turn them against the European idea itself. The still fragile gains, which are favourable to a gradual implementation of this idea, would then be themselves swiftly eroded.

That is really a nightmare scenario. People who are optimistic by temperament might say that Europe has seen off similar disasters in the past. But although it is true that the societies of this continent have no reason to be ashamed of their history, and that in the end they have always cleared a path to progress, they have often paid a high price in their own blood, as the struggle of democracy against fascism illustrates powerfully.

Europe is not threatened from without. Nor was it between 1945 and 1990, even if certain political forces stoked up a largely illusory fear of the USSR and Communism. To suggest that it might be threatened today by the peoples and states of the South, and particularly by Islamic fundamentalism, borders on the grotesque. The wretched options that may now and again carry the day in the South will cause victims only among their own peoples and nations, serving to increase their backwardness, and therefore their weakness, on the world arena.

Europe is threatened from within. For its western part, the threat does not look as if it can go beyond a certain threshold of dramatic intensity. The well-known conflicts traditionally classified as national or communal – Ireland, Spain and Belgium being the main theatres – will not necessarily worsen or remain unresolved. And it is rather hard to imagine that the major conflicts of the past among the region's large powers (Britain, France, Germany) can revive and take the form of European wars. In the East, on the other hand, the dramatic threshold has already been crossed. The absurdity of neoliberal 'reconversion' policies is fuelling a social and economic catastrophe, which could challenge the credibility of the democratic gains and make them appear a purely passing phenomenon. Local political forces are, to be sure, the first ones responsible for the violent crises shaking the region in response to its spiral of involution. But the responsibility is shared with the states of Western Europe. Will they throw water or oil on the fire? So far, they have done the latter, in practice if not intentionally. By supporting the centrifugal tendencies inevitably generated by neoliberal chaos, Western diplomatic action has everywhere thrown oil on the fire – encouraged by demagogues at bay who are seeking a new (ethnic) basis to legitimize their rule. It was absolutely obvious that historical constructions such as the USSR or Yugoslavia were not going to crumble without unleashing murderous conflicts. It was obvious that the first confused elections expressed nothing other than disorientation. Europe did not choose to help the forces seeking the victory of patience, which in many cases might have been capable of stemming the violence of the initial reactions. I would note here that Germany appears to have been the driving force in Europe's destructive intervention. It unilaterally recognized the independence of Slovenia and Croatia, and a month later the Community endorsed its decision. This was no doubt the sign of a (German or European?) project in the making: to Latin Americanize Eastern Europe.

In the short term, this project of national break-up and social disaggregation fits into the utopian vision of 'running the world like a market', which means to fragment power as much as possible, to deprive states of all effectiveness, in the face of a ubiquitous market.

Since there is no longer an iron curtain, however, developments in one half of Europe have direct effects on the other half. And as we know, a bad example is often stronger than a good. Associated with the deepening crisis in the West, the new fascisms in the East encourage the resurgent ones in the West. But apart from that danger, which happily is still only marginal, the chaos is promoting the revival of state nationalisms. If the countries of Europe together have nothing convincing to offer, the temptation will be stronger to seek national, and nationalist, solutions, in which case Europe will unintentionally find itself back in the nineteenth century, when conflict between nations was just as much to the fore as the class struggle.

For the building of Europe is no more inevitable than Arab unity, the triumph of pan-Africanism or Latin American integration. Centrifugal tendencies also exist and operate in Europe, including its Western half.

And for each European nation, there are other options besides continental unity.

For a long time, Britain was more preoccupied with maintaining Commonwealth ties, inherited from its imperial hegemony, than with its own possible integration into Europe. After 1945 it made a choice that it never abandoned: to make unconditional alliance with the United States its top priority. So far, it has been possible to reconcile this with membership of the European Community. But what of the future, if the rivalry between Europe and the United States becomes more intense? Or if Europe were to fly into pieces? Or if Germany were to dominate Europe?

In 1945–46 France set out to revive its Empire within an associationist framework (an association of independent nations, or of nations destined to become independent in the serious sense of the term). Colonialist forces emptied the project of its capacity for renewal, however, and managed to keep colonial relations in place until – to the detriment of the old declining colonial interests, and in favour of dynamic modernizing sectors – changes within French capitalism gave France a shove in the direction of European integration. Today it no longer has any other choice. But that is an element of weakness, precisely because the main European power, Germany, enjoys much greater room for manoeuvre.

After 1871 Germany developed a project of its own: the *Drang nach Osten*, the push eastward. Has it given this up? Of course, Germany has become a democracy after the fashion of Britain and France, which was not really true of Bismarck's Second Reich, and certainly not of Hitler's odious Third Reich. Because they appreciate the crucial importance of this gain, democratic forces in that country are convinced that a 'European Germany' is preferable to a 'German Europe', as they put it. The fact is, however, that the Fourth Reich is already with us, as we can see plainly enough from its intervention in Yugoslavia, from the disturbing resurrection of the 'Sudeten question', and from many other signs. Is a democratic Fourth Reich possible? Why not? British imperialism and French imperialism spread their wings without calling into question bourgeois democracy in the metropolis. A democratic Fourth Reich might even take up the objectives of the *Drang nach Osten* in a way that does not appear intolerable to the peoples of Eastern Europe: a regional hegemony, that is, operating through economics as US hegemony does at a world level (also without its democracy being destroyed). Germany certainly has a lot of room for manoeuvre; it might be able to pursue an Eastern policy of its own without challenging the construction of Europe, and its partners (France, above all) would be forced to endorse its initiatives. Such a 'German Europe' would, of course, locate itself within an 'American universe', because Germany would not commit the mistake (which was Hitler's undoing) of biting off more than it could chew.

For the time being, the possible choices of other Community members do not have the same import. But it does look as if Italy, Spain, Belgium, the Netherlands and the Scandinavian countries would accept a German Europe without too much difficulty, especially if Germany pursues its strategy without giving up democracy.

Could Russia be kept out of things forever? What of the countries of the ex-USSR liable to be coveted by Moscow or by others (Germany in the case of the Baltic states and Ukraine)? Here too the short-term option is playing the game of the *Drang nach Osten*. For Germany's ideas of expansion will be limited at first to Austria (already part of its area), the Czech Republic (now undergoing compradorization), Slovenia, Croatia, Hungary, Poland, the Baltic states and the Ukraine.

I will conclude this nightmare scenario by saying that it seems destined to revive a nineteenth-century Europe – either an Anglo-Franco-Russian alliance to contain German ambitions, or a new German-Russian carve-up that would finally isolate France.

A Different Future: A Radical Vision for Europe

5. Most fortunately, the nightmare scenario is not the only one imaginable. There is also a progressive scenario, even though a great deal would be required for it to be successful.

The European project cannot rest content with 'managing democracy in a multinational area'. The lowest common denominator is quite inadequate: it is even incapable of protecting the Community's economic gains or simply Europe's democratic achievements. The crisis – which is not a recession but a structural (more than just economic) crisis of society – may seriously erode the legitimacy of the European democratic tradition itself.

Faced with a series of challenges (what kind of development for Europe? How to reconcile this with globalization? How to reconcile nations and supranationality within Europe itself?), the European project will not find answers unless it comes up with a genuine plan for society that measures up to the problems of our age. I will therefore conclude by listing the dimensions of any societal project worthy of the name.

(1) A project for society is first of all a social vision, a way of conceiving social relations. This cannot be just an implicit result

of the reproduction of the productive system. It has to be explicit in the actuality of social relations, which are partly (in their hard core) class relations operating on the basis of productive systems, but partly also relations in other fields of reality (relations between men and women, for example). The procedure of making the project explicit at these levels may be described as a social contract – I see no special problem in calling it so. We already know of a historical precedent that underpinned the European (and American) miracle: namely, the national historic compromise between capital and labour, in which the state played an indispensable role as site of negotiation and instrument of implementation. There can be no question of a remake of this model; its time has passed, if only because of the processes of globalization and European integration themselves. Nevertheless, the social contract comes before, and not after, the economic strategies deployed within its framework, or upon its foundation. Conventional economists have difficulty in accepting this order of precedence: they have always thought – perhaps as a result of economistic alienation – that the economy decides everything. There is no point, either, in pinning the label 'capitalist' or 'socialist' to the social relations defining the project. I say this not because the two concepts are meaningless or have lost their historical significance; on the contrary, they are still full of both. But the long transition from world capitalism to world socialism implies the conflictual coexistence of capitalist logics (for example, market, profit calculation, work hierarchy) and anti-capitalist logics (justice and democracy as natural products not of capitalist expansion, but of the struggle of peoples against the one-sided logic of capital accumulation).

(2) Beyond the social contract regulating the conditions of reproduction of the productive system, a project for society that measures up to the requirements of our age implies a vision of the future of our technological civilization. The question of the future of work is now posed. After the mass-worker of the Fordist epoch, the citizen-worker-intellectual is tending to form the new mass in the productive system of tomorrow. This will be based upon computerized and automated technologies, with all that they imply for interdependence between all segments of the system and for the questioning of the hitherto dominant forms of the law of value (which is what economists, with their characteristic naïvety, refer to when they talk about 'the technological factor'

as the principal and ultimate determinant of productivity). Does not the new type of worker required for this system suggests the replacement of the wage with 'citizenship income'? It also seems obvious that the ecological challenge – which cannot be internalized in the short-term horizons of conventional cost calculation – is posing the problems of economic decision-making in new terms. 'Workers' participation' or German-style 'joint management' are, of course, far from solving such problems, which raise the whole question of the nature of our civilization. The future of ownership, and of the new forms we should be moving towards, are a challenge for every dimension of social thought and action.

(3) Is it necessary to point out that the historical concepts underpinning national solidarity are the very ones that have been called into question by the challenge of 'supranationality' – most obviously with regard to European integration, but in other areas too? How are difference, specificity and universalism to be reconceptualized within this new framework?

(4) At a directly political level, the European project is faced with the question of relations between Europe and the United States, which have so far been framed by the NATO military alliance. As the enemy against which this alliance was supposedly forged is no longer with us, what is the purpose of NATO's continuation? Is it to deal with a new adversary – Islam, perhaps, or the Asians? Feverish attempts are being made to put together something out of nothing, by hastily constructing a theory of 'conflict between cultures' which carries conviction only with those already convinced. For what about the fact that this adversary does not pose any military threat? One of the replies most often heard – that NATO has become the instrument or spearhead for democratization of the world – is so reminiscent of the old 'civilizing mission' that it should be greeted with spontaneous laughter. Again, one can only laugh when one looks with anything more than infantile naïvety at the military interventions of our time (the Gulf War for democracy in Kuwait!). In reality, NATO is part of the arsenal needed for political management of the chaos resulting from the economic side of capitalist management. So long as Europe does not aim to move beyond this crisis, it can only knuckle under to American military hegemony. But such an option, by perpetuating

America's world hegemony, destroys much of the significance that has been ascribed to Europe's new economic competition with the United States, destroys, in fact, much of the European dream of 'independence'.

(5) The European project, it is hardly necessary to repeat, is in direct conflict with the Latin Americanization of the eastern half of the continent. I tried above to explain why and how the latter will blow the former apart.

(6) Finally, can the European project simply echo the hollow discourse of economists obsessed with the appearances of Third World 'marginalization'? Can it really ignore the South at the very moment when access to the natural resources of the whole planet has become more vital than ever for the survival of 'the West'? This question of access could, it is true, be regulated by a global neo-imperialism. But apart from the fact that this would inevitably be the best way of perpetuating the hegemony of the so-called American competitor, can anyone seriously think for a moment that it would prove viable? A quite different approach would be to consider the ways in which the large regional areas (Europe, Latin America, Africa, the Arab world) need to mesh together with the continental powers (US, China, India) in a relationship of interdependence favourable to their own development and capable of reducing the effects of polarization inherent in globalization through the market. I have developed some ideas elsewhere (as shown in Chapter 5) on these matters, and I will not go over them again here.

To sum up, the six themes raised here constitute, in my view, an agenda that falls logically into the tradition of left-wing thinking about movements and progress. If this is so, either Europe will be of the Left or it will not be at all.

References

Casanova, P. G. (ed.), *Etat et Politique dans le Tiers Monde*, L'Harmattan, Paris, 1994

CHAPTER 7

Ideology and Social Thought: The Intelligentsia and the Development Crisis

Social Theory and the Critique of Capitalism: Marxism, Postmodernism and the Social Movements

I use the term 'social thought' (or 'social theory') advisedly, in preference to 'social science', so as to avoid the spurious identification of analytical social disciplines with the natural sciences. I think the presumption that the former could ever attain the epistemological status of the latter is overweening. For one thing, were any social discipline to rival the natural sciences in power, even to a relative degree, such a development would be harmful. It would reduce social governance to the level of livestock management, and thus abolish human liberty. Human/social liberation, and the twin objective of control over nature (both understood, again, as relative constructs) necessarily imply resistance to the pretensions of self-styled rational management even when such claims are backed by social disciplines hyped up as scientific, objective and therefore effective.

It is, of course, a long-standing ambition of bourgeois thought – which postmodernist critics confuse with modern thought – to make the social disciplines as rigorously scientific as the natural sciences. The social system that serves as bedrock for bourgeois thought (in plain terms, the capitalist system), seen in this context, is a product of a worldview most clearly expressed in the economic sphere. Weber, who is enjoying a revival these days, presented this self-image of capitalist society in a formula of astounding naïvety: capitalism, he argued, entailed the triumph of a rational ethos working to liberate the world from the thralldom of age-old irrational norms.

For some time now I've been suggesting an alternative view of the contrast between past thought systems and modern (capitalist) thought.

My comparative approach is based on the contrast in emphasis between precapitalist societies (I call them tributary societies), with their stress on metaphysical aspects of reality, and capitalist societies, with their stress on economic aspects. From this novel point of view, the difference between the metaphysical worldview of tributary societies and the thinking of a more advanced society due to evolve after resolving the economistic biases and contradictions of the bourgeois system, need not be so sharply oppositional. We might call such an advanced society socialist.

By enshrining its new economic rationality as an absolute value, bourgeois thought sought to legitimize the emergent form of social organization. In the process, it assumed the new organizational form to be an eternal construct somehow signalling, as certain commentators have written quite recently, again with extraordinary naïvety, the end of history. This was a worldview in which Progress (with a capital P) became a surrogate for God, the basis of an everlasting scheme of things.

From our viewpoint, there were two aspects in which capitalism and bourgeois thought, despite their limitations, represented a measure of progress (with a lower-case p). They birthed forces which initiated prodigious material development, achieving unprecedented control over nature. We should remember, though, that this control has by no means been entirely positive: it now poses a threat to the survival of the planet. Simultaneously, by freeing social ideas from old metaphysical prejudices, capitalism and bourgeois thought prepared the way for the concept and the modern practice of democracy. Here again we should point out that such democratic practice was circumscribed by the very nature of the system. The equation of the market (as synecdoche for capitalist reality) with democracy is of course unduly facile. But it is based on this real, tangible instance of progress.

The critique of capitalism is meaningless unless it sharpens our awareness of these limitations of bourgeois thought. To do this it must examine capitalism both as a qualitatively new stage of historical development and as an instance of the unfolding of contradictions between the liberating aspirations the new system encourages and its inability to satisfy those aspirations on the scale of its own creation – the global society. The critique of capitalism aims unambiguously to transcend capitalism. That means it must be ready to transcend modernity interpreted as a simile for capitalism. To achieve that aim, the critique of capitalism should also put forward alternative rules for social organization, along with alternative values. In short, it has to present an alternative system of rationality. Does that mean the critique of capitalism will, like capitalism itself before it, inevitably be tempted to present the new rationality of its own creative utopia as an eternal construct? I think the new critique can avoid that lapse.

But has the critique of capitalism truly outgrown the existing framework of bourgeois thought? That is the question. For the moment it cannot be given a cut-and-dried answer. The new critique is still incomplete. It needs to be deepened and enriched with insights generated from its interaction with new challenges thrown up by the very development of capitalism. Initially focused on moral values, the critique of capitalism reached what I maintain was a decisive stage in the work of Karl Marx. At that juncture Marxism went through a series of gradual developments under the Second and then the Third International. Along the way it assimilated the economistic bias of bourgeois theory, yielded to the lure of its deterministic vision, and thus turned the 'laws of history' into a set of implacable rules identical to the inexorable laws of the natural sciences. Marxism thus ended up advocating, in the name of socialism, a utopian system of rationalized management based on knowledge of these 'laws', and in that process trashed the dialectic of human freedom.

Marxism, then, is by any measure obviously incomplete. Nevertheless, it would be totally unjust to reduce it to a particular form, that of Soviet ideology, which I have long considered as closer to bourgeois thought than to Marxist thinking.

The critique of capitalism antedated the faddish critique now offered us by postmodernist theoreticians. The point is to judge whether postmodernist theory contributes any fresh insights. I consider postmodernism an intellectual non-starter, in the sense that beyond its hype it offers no conceptual instruments capable of transcending the capitalist framework; neither does it demonstrate any capacity to inspire an innovative design for social change. In short, the postmodernist critique is less radical than the critique whose seminal ideas were put forward in Marx's work.

No doubt the exercises in the deconstruction of discourse whereby Lyotard, Derrida, Deleuze, Guattari, Foucault and Baudrillard laid the groundwork for postmodernism (in the form advocated by American scholars and by Touraine in France) did serve some useful purpose. They had the merit of exposing the metaphysical nature both of post-Enlightenment bourgeois discourse and of its extension in the prevailing schools of socialist thought. They laid bare the essentialist bias of that discourse, that is to say, its option in favour of metaphysical explanations, in its search for the absolute. They shed light on its economistic prejudices, which subordinated every aspect of social life to the imperatives of economic rationality. They made explicit its implicit teleological thrust, according to which historical laws work with implacable rigidity in the steady onward march of Progress.

The insights of such postmodernists may therefore look fresh to readers previously impressed by the assumptions of bourgeois essentialism, economism and teleology. For those who never swallowed such assumptions, however, they represent nothing fresher than one more trip along the boundaries of bourgeois thought. And on that itinerary the pioneer, in my opinion, was Marx.

Postmodernist thinkers, as we know, rediscovered that the Enlightenment did not liberate humanity. From the standpoint of the precise strain of Marxist thinking that I share, that is merely axiomatic. Our school of Marxist theory highlights the realization that the economistic alienation peculiar to bourgeois ideology (including its so-called socialist variants) is an extension of – and a functional surrogate for – the metaphysical alienation typical of past worldviews, in the same way as capitalist exploitation is an extension of and a surrogate for tributary exploitation. So when Lyotard says Auschwitz and Stalin meant the failure of the modernist dream, his laconic formula leaves out an adjective: capitalist. For imperialism and its virulent offspring, fascism, along with world wars and colonial massacres, are all precisely a product of sharpening contradictions within the capitalist system, a measure of the conflict between the promises of freedom it holds out and its inability to deliver commensurate improvements. The Soviet ideology itself, with its economistic vision focused on 'catching up' (signifying, in my opinion, a dream of capitalism without capitalists), was a variation of bourgeois ideology. As such, as Maoist thinkers predicted 35 years ago, it was scheduled in the course of its natural development to lead to 'normal' capitalism. Events over the past several years, in themselves hardly surprising, have borne out that prediction.

The postmodernist critique, pitched short of the radical perspectives attained by Marxist thought, fails to provide the tools needed to transcend capitalism. For that reason, its propositions remain ambiguous, hazy. Its penchant for the uncritical adulation of difference and the glorification of empiricism make it quite compatible with conventional, economistic management practices designed to perpetuate capitalist practices, still considered the definitive, eternal expression of rationality. That leaves the way open for neoconservative communalist ideologies of the kind common in Anglo-Saxon traditions of social management. In extreme cases, it may also lead to nihilistic explosions. Either way, the result is an ideology compatible with the interests of the privileged, those whom Galbraith, in his brilliant analysis, calls the 'haves'.

Still, the emphasis on the need for democracy is far from pointless. It might, in fact, turn out to be an effective stimulus for new advances in the theoretical and practical critique of capitalism, assuming the concept of democracy is understood in all its dynamic scope. Workers' struggles gave depth and meaning to democracy in past times; in much the same way, we should not overlook the possibility that the struggle for democracy might impart a progressive spin to the course of coming events. That, as a matter of fact, is a hope shared by a substantial section of the postmodernist school. It is not my intention to accuse them of harbouring 'evolutionary' illusions doomed to frustration from the start. For I maintain that the dichotomy established between evolution, misconstrued as betrayal, and revolution, presented as the sole acceptable path of socialist transition, was a specific result of circumstances linked to the world wars and the Russian Revolution, not a logical inference from the radical critique of capitalism. In the particular conditions of the time such an interpretation might have reflected reality accurately enough. But then what began as an expedient interpretation was subsequently raised to the level of an absolute principle by vulgar Marxists – an unwarranted shift. Similarly, the role assigned to the working class may well have been an accurate reflection of the real function of that class under the objective conditions created by capitalism at an earlier stage of its development. But it now needs to be revised in the light of changes in the capitalist system resulting from the interplay of social forces both in their national environments and on the world scale. For some time now, strategies for a revolutionary break with capitalism have been pushed backstage. That does not mean there is no longer any need to transcend the capitalist system. All it means is that the time is ripe for the design of new strategies sophisticated enough to encompass current changes within the capitalist system itself.

The fact remains that the rejection of Marxism is fashionable these days. To facilitate such rejection, Marxism is first reduced to its Soviet manifestation, then condemned for 'explanatory overkill', by which is meant a tendency to explain reality in terms of a deterministic scheme which makes every event not only explainable but also the necessary outcome of the laws of capitalist development. Many Marxists may deserve this accusation. When levelled at Marx himself, however, it is patently unjust.

Meanwhile the issue of the relation between the economic and non-economic spheres, that is to say, of links between politics and culture, remains unsettled both within the Marxist framework as so far developed, and within other theoretical frameworks including the postmodernist scheme. The economistic idea according to which culture adjusts to economic imperatives does not come from Marx. Instead, it reflects prevalent bourgeois ideological perceptions from the Enlightenment to this day. But the contrary notion of cultures as nucleic constants, peddled by the now modish cultural pluralists, some of them simply Eurocentric, some reverse Eurocentrists, seems to me even less tenable, even flimsier in the face of reality, if that is possible. What then of a middle position between these extremes, dictated perhaps by prudence (*in medio stat virtus*)? How satisfactory might it be, and how would it operate? The fact is that certain thinkers have in the past adopted just such an attitude yet shed no useful light on the issue. Weber is a good example. His theses, in particular those on the Protestant ethic and the rise of capitalism, seem to me rather unconvincing if not downright weak.

Similarly, the issue of the dynamics of social conflict, a simpler problem at first glance, has within the Marxist tradition itself continued to raise questions eluding definitive answers. How, for example, does a class-in-itself turn into a class-for-itself? We know that on this issue Lenin advanced a set of propositions asserting that theory is imported into the working class from external sources, an argument others have described as non-Marxist. And how, for instance, does Gramsci's organic intellectual group emerge? Needless to say, any progress in the solution of these problems presupposes advances in our understanding of relationships between the economic, political and cultural spheres. Here again we might choose to stay on solid empirical ground and observe that there are many social actors, to use the term in vogue; that their plans, implicit or explicit, are piecemeal and cover domains naturally different from each other; that there is therefore no way to predict whether they will complement each other or clash, whether they are feasible or utopian; and that for these reasons the outcome of their confrontations is impossible to forecast.

Thus formulated, all this is axiomatic. But it seems to me illogical to argue from these premises that 'social movements' (invariably plural), because they are vectors of social change, and because they express the aspirations of real human groups, all deserve respect and support in the spirit of democratic equity. Why should we respect and support any group if we have no idea where its plans may lead? Why exclude the possibility that established regimes may manipulate them? It seems to me that many of the ethnic claims advanced these days are subject to manipulation by governments more concerned with crisis management than with solving underlying problems. Such governments may manipulate a people's right to self-determination not in order to increase its freedom but to curtail it. So the option of 'activism in the service of movements', an approach supposedly based on the analysis of social actors, carries the risk of an anti-theoretical bias no less dangerous than its opposite, the prejudice of dogmatic theory.

The Intelligentsia *vis-à-vis* Mental Operatives

The social sciences comprise a range of loosely integrated skills and methods applicable to the analysis of social reality. The epistemological status of these disciplines varies widely from field to field. In economics, the prevailing obsession with management has imposed an agenda of specific issues, a selective approach to significant data, and a tunnel vision of reality focused narrowly on management goals. True, such options sometimes enhance efficiency. But then the so-called science of economics implies a latent ideological option that legitimizes the kind of management involved, and by extension the social system it perpetuates, namely the capitalist system. For that reason the discipline of economics sidesteps more basic issues related to social change and historical development, assigning them to the free play of imaginative thinking, a process it considers unscientific.

Marx sought, successfully, I think, to expose the alienation engendered by capitalist society, by whose workings 'economic laws' are supposed to operate 'as inexorably as' natural laws, a ploy that enhances the practical managerial efficiency of the system to a perceptible degree. He shifted the issues raised from this narrow domain of system maintenance to the much broader field of social change. Despite this shift, however, a Marxian tradition in the analysis of the capitalist economy did develop, whose approach was close to that of the economistic school, notably in its definition of problems.

In any case the radical critique of capitalism formulated by Marx contains no definitive solutions to problems related to the management of a society liberated from economistic dogma. Neither does it offer a panacea for the transition to such a society. These issues came to the fore the moment revolutionary social movements took over political power and set about building socialism. Given objective conditions at the time, their plans were tinged with ambiguity. What was the goal: to construct socialism, or to catch up with advanced capitalism? This uncertainty was no doubt at the root of certain options regarding the management of the transition, such as the adoption of an administrative command economy in place of a market economy. These options were then rationalized by an invocation of rationality (the construction of a society managed by scientific reason) typical of bourgeois ideology. It was this kind of rationalization that had provoked Engels's criticism of the German Social-Democrats when he called their plans a dream of 'capitalism without capitalists'.

In my opinion these issues are still unresolved. For the worldwide polarization inherent in capitalism implies a need for long-range strategies for the transition, taking full account of a somewhat contradictory agenda: on the one hand, the need to build up productive forces; on the other, the need to design alternative social relationships. The debate on these strategies, especially regarding their economic aspect (the social management of the market) is therefore still wide open.

Social thought, in short, cannot be penned up within the confines into which the economistic school would like to push it. But there is no way we can separate the urge to understand society as a whole from the desire to direct its evolution one way or another. Ideology (the value system underpinning the advocacy of a particular social design) and science (knowledge of objective functional realities affecting change) are here inseparable. I think, for instance, that the concept of development is an ideological concept defined by the design of the type of society the development process is supposed to bring about. And as I have tried constantly to make clear, development should not be confused with the realities of the modern world. Those realities are geared not to development but to the expansion of capitalism. The fact that the gurus, politicians and managers playing the current development game routinely blur this crucial distinction merely underlines their commitment to a latent capitalist design. Similarly, feminists have entirely exposed the ideological bases of established social 'science'. They have showed how, through the definition of issues (what is significant, what is marginal?) and through the selective use of methodologies serving established definitions of reality, that social disciplines manage to push feminist questions outside the framework of investigation, because the social aims subtending the disciplines are geared to the perpetuation of the patriarchal system.

The foregoing reflections in turn call for the clear differentiation of social thinkers according to the social aims driving their work. On the one hand, there are those Galbraith calls the 'haves'. From their viewpoint all our society needs is managers (of the capitalist system, of course, understood as a system capable of changing in hopefully positive directions, still to be defined). Anything beyond that frame presents, according to these 'haves', a public danger. On the other hand there are those who say our society's overriding need is for critical thinking leading to a better understanding of the mechanisms of change, and therefore able to influence such change in ways that will free society from capitalist alienation and its tragic consequences. As far as the overwhelming majority of humanity – the peoples of Asia, Africa and Latin America –

are concerned, this need is vital, since they experience actually existing capitalism as nothing short of savagery.

The distinction I propose here, then, separates those whom I call operatives, serving the established ideological apparatus, from the intelligentsia proper. The latter has no impact except to the extent that it is critical and competent. In other words, it has to be capable of inspiring liberating action within a sustained programme of linked theory and practice. From this perspective, any assessment of the output of Third World intellectuals, including that of African intellectuals, ought to start from an analysis of the relationship between the challenges faced by their peoples in the confrontation with 'actually existing capitalism', and the orientation of the actions inspired by their work. I shall return later to a more concrete interpretation of the kind of assessment proposed here.

Development: Contrasting Critiques

Now that the critique of development has become a live issue, I think the time has come to examine the types of criticism levelled at the concept and practice of the postwar development scheme; to conduct a critical assessment of theories, concepts and practices attendant on the process now in its crisis-ridden state; to review new analytical techniques used by these critics; and to evaluate the strategies they propose.

Critiques of development fall into two schools. According to the first school, in the palmy days from the 1950s to the 1970s, the experience of development, however uneven, was on the whole positive. Since then, the process has stalled. The point therefore is to kick-start it once more. According to these critics, the cause of the stall is the general crisis affecting the developed centres of the world economy. Some trace the root of this crisis to the development policies followed, considered excessively nationalistic, and for that reason incompatible with the imperatives of globalization. Others see the problem as the result of the combined impact of the two processes. Obviously, such critics still consider development coterminous with the worldwide expansion of capitalism. From their viewpoint the development process is a sort of natural outcome of capitalism, though some would add that capitalist expansion needs to be channelled along adequate policy guidelines, so as to plane down its rough edges. In short, such criticism remains bounded within the parameters of the managerial approach.

Then there are critics of an opposite school who think the development process under discussion is in crisis because it has defaulted on its promises; because it has led to increasingly unequal patterns of income distribution between societies on this planet and within societies on the periphery of the system, in the process worsening the poverty and marginalization of the disadvantaged instead of integrating all social strata into a steadily inclusive and more stable system; and because it has produced a dangerous waste of non-renewable resources and provoked a horrific devastation of the environment. Our own concerns coincide largely with such critiques. It might be helpful, then, at this stage, to point out that articulate criticism of the development ethos antedated the crisis of the 1980s. And that brings us to the need to recapitulate the ideas of critics of the development process in its heyday.

I am well aware that current criticisms of past critiques of development vary in type and scope, and that any attempt to file them down to a few general statements will only compromise the clarity of ongoing debates. I shall therefore do my best not to overgeneralize. However, it seems to me that quite often, our critics present skewed summaries of our arguments, then lump them together under the general label of 'Neo-Marxism in Recent Decades', which they present as a body of thought in a state of crisis. As a matter of fact, most frequently our critics have themselves been members of one or another such neo-Marxist school, and the criticisms and self-criticisms advanced by some of them have been inspired by the same preoccupations as in the past.

In this recurrent presentation, neo-Marxist schools of thought are in turn classified under three main categories depending on whether their theoretical emphasis is on modes of production, dependence or the world system. The analyses presented are of course varied, with key stresses differing from author to author. But I confess I am in agreement with a great many of the criticisms most frequently raised against these neo-Marxist schools. I think, for instance, that the perennial fine-tuning of concepts related to modes of production is an expression of a donnish obsession with detail more likely to obscure real issues than to clarify them. Further, it seems to me that theories developed within the framework of dependency or that of the world system have sometimes been mechanistic, economistic, deterministic. The list of reservations could go on.

Valid as these criticisms are, however, I think no purpose is served by flushing the baby down the drain with the bathwater. It would be useful to keep a clear focus on what in my view are important contributions of the neo-Marxist thinking under discussion. One such achievement is the highlighting of links between the national and world spheres. All subsequent modifications of this theoretical insight have shown that it was of vital importance, and that it served as an antidote to the naïve approaches of the ideologues and theorists of both the bourgeois and the dominant Marxist schools.

That said, let me point out that I do not see my work as belonging to any of these schools. I am certain I am not alone in this case, further proof of the limitations of this artificial kind of categorization. My constant focus on historical materialism, understood in its totality, with special reference to the history of, and the transition to, capitalism, my criticism of the economistic and Eurocentric vision of dominant meta-theories in these fields, were at the very least an expression of a determination to avoid the kind of faults now imputed – sometimes justifiably – to the neo-Marxist schools: their economistic and essentialist bias, their often sophomoric and dogmatic interpretations of Marxism, and their teleological tendencies, particularly obvious in the Soviet strain of vulgar Marxism.

The gist of my critique of the critical corpus, however, falls outside the scope of so-called theoretical works. For social thought, is inseparable from the practical work it inspires. I would therefore rather examine and re-examine statements and analyses put forward within the framework of neo-Marxist critiques of development by situating the underlying environment in which they were formulated. This was the task I set myself in a recent re-examination of 'The Unfolding and Erosion of the Bandung Plan' in *Re-reading the Post-War Period*, where I emphasized challenges facing theoretical thinkers on account of the impact of real-life conflicts. In this framework there is no way anyone can overlook past Soviet formulations, the rival formulations of Maoist thought, and the ambiguous stances of radical populist Third World nationalism, which has, alas, petered out completely in the current analysis of past critiques of the development process. I find this intellectual penury deplorable, and I think that this serious lacuna is an outcome of the ivory-tower nature of most of these criticisms. I think a further contributing factor has been the U-turn executed by many Western left-wing intellectuals, in their retreat from a characteristically naïve enthusiasm for the Third World to a pro-imperialist stance now hardly distinguishable from Third World-bashing.

The main argument used in this self-criticism of Third World advocacy is that, given the wide range of developmental paths, it was foolhardy to insist on comprehensive assessments of capitalism on a world scale, to focus on the contrast between centres and peripheries, and to highlight imperialism. That, supposedly, was the fatal flaw in Marxism, shared by neo-Marxism as well. For the diverse reality in question necessarily called for a subtly differentiated analysis capable of accounting seriously for internal circumstances governing the development of each society at all levels (economic, political, cultural), and thus determining the evolution – progressive or regressive – of each society within the world system.

Formulated thus, the argument strikes me as a truism. At no point in our analyses have I (or any authors whose perspectives I share) claimed that the worldwide expansion of capitalism levelled all differences. Quite the contrary: all our efforts were focused on analysing the nature and scope of differentiations occurring in the process of that expansion, precisely on account of the interface between the general(or world) and the particular (or national) aspects of reality. The acknowledgement of diversity, perfectly normal in itself, does not absolve us from the parallel necessity to recognize the general. For in the absence of the general, diversity is meaningless. The real issue raised by diversity lies elsewhere, and it is often misperceived by the critics referred to here: does modernization within the capitalist framework lead to 'catching up', that is to say, to the abolition of worldwide polarization? And if so, does the outcome depend on internal national conditions?

Now as in the past, implicitly or explicitly, the question draws two opposite responses. Yes, according to some, no, according to others. I share the latter view. Meanwhile, these polarized positions take on new forms in keeping with the new configuration of the capitalist system, different from that of the postwar boom years (1945–90).

There are other critiques, set in a framework fundamentally different from the Marxist or neo-Marxist tradition, and in explicit disagreement therewith. Postmodernist criticism, as we have already seen, belongs to this category. As a matter of fact, it would be accurate to say that the Third World does not interest postmodernist thinkers, because they see it as a mere collection of backward states, in line with the bourgeois worldview, past and present. Some postmodernists are in the habit of projecting trends they discern in the developed world on to social movements within the peripheral countries. In my opinion, their extrapolations have little to do with reality. For far from expressing a rejection of modernity, the movements in question are in fact the consequence of the shattering of the promise of real modernization, a failure typical of peripheral capitalism.

The various development strategies, often hastily hyped up as new when the only novelty they present is their packaging, remain vague and short of credibility. The repeated calls for democracy, given a high profile in contemporary discourse by practically unanimous consent, is certainly a positive change. It should at least help demolish such wrong-headed but widespread prejudices as the supposition that democracy follows automatically from development. For those of us who see development as a shorthand term for a progressive social design, the democratization of society is by definition an integral part of the development process. Without it the objective of liberation and the effective exercise of power by the people is reduced to empty theory.

Agreement with this viewpoint, however, does not mean the problem is solved. Beyond that, we also need to analyse the practical ways in which peripheral capitalism acts as an objective obstacle blocking the path to democracy. That, incidentally, is why anti-democratic prejudices have characterized the approaches not only of so-called socialist technocrats but also those of overtly capitalist establishments, a clear indication that real development clashes with the imperatives of capitalist expansion. Lastly, we have to be able to design practical action programmes linking democratization with social advancement, with sufficient courage to implement effective policies within such a framework and to deal boldly with the risk of conflict that arises from the thrust of capitalist expansion. (It is this option that I call delinking.)

Other strategic options currently in fashion, such as advances in women's liberation, increased cultural awareness and concern with the environment, are certainly, on their merits, undeniably important. Unfortunately, rhetorical outpourings on these issues are still often ambiguous and superficial. Development agencies have become extraordinarily clever in handling these matters, changing their rhetoric without ever challenging established regimes. There is constant talk of 'women in development', of respect for cultural values, of sustainable development. But rarely does anyone take the trouble to conduct a preliminary analysis of relationships nurtured by the expansionist capitalist system as far as male and female roles, extant cultural values or the reproduction of the natural conditions of production are concerned.

Any design for development as a liberating process is bound to throw up extremely complex issues in these areas. And the typical evasive arrogance of development managers is a totally inadequate response. Here too the connection between the universal (especially the universalistic objective of necessarily worldwide transformation) and the particular (which defines the stages of transition) raises a series of theoretical and practical dilemmas. Instead of facing them, development managers with their frothy rhetoric simply and shamelessly sidestep these problems.

Under these conditions, strategic proposals put forward in scattershot fashion run a high risk of getting turned into simple crisis-management strategems, instead of serving as pointers to a resolution of the crisis. The risk is especially high since the managerial élite is not above manipulating potentially progressive but incoherently organized proposals, turning them into slogans helpful to established regimes.

The Analyses and Strategies put forward by the Third World Intelligentsia

My intention, then, is to examine the analyses and strategies put forward by the Third World intelligentsia, and in particular by the African intelligentsia, during the past several decades, and to interpret them, clarifying linkages between them and the real-life stakes involved in the liberation struggles of the time. I intend to conduct a similar assessment of the debate about ongoing transformations on the scale of the world system and of the various African systems, as a way of identifying pointers to new stakes and appropriate strategies.

I propose an analysis of the half century following the Second World War (1945–90) as a long phase in the expansion of ascendant capitalism. That analysis will be rooted in the modular system mentioned in Chapter 3 (p. 46): the national social-democratic compromise in the developed Western countries; the Soviet design for catching up with the West within a framework of disengagement; and the bourgeois nationalist development scheme to which I have given the name the Bandung Project (see *Empire of Chaos*, and *Intellectual Itinerary*). The steady erosion of the systems built on these bases, culminating in their collapse, has led to a phase of long-term structural crisis on the world scale. Meanwhile, the deepening process of globalization, which caused the erosion of the now outmoded systems in the first place, has resulted in a new definition of worldwide capitalist polarization. By the same token it has defined the parameters of new challenges facing those committed to liberation struggles.

Within this optic, it is necessary to re-examine the analyses and strategies put forward by the Third World and African intelligentsia in the postwar period as expressions of the process I have called 'the unfolding and erosion of the Bandung Project'. What that Project entailed was a bourgeois-nationalist modernization scheme designed to lead to the construction of relatively endocentric and industrialized national economies within an internal framework of controlled interdependence on the world scale, as opposed to the Soviet framework of disengagement. Needless to say, there were numerous variations of this Project, depending on internal factors, in particular the degree of radicalization of the anti-imperialist liberation front, in much the same way as achievements in the liberation struggle, as measured by effective industrialization and competitiveness, have turned out to be uneven, depending on internal and external factors.

The way I see it, throughout the past half-century the main divide between the principal opponents in this debate in the Third World and Africa was defined by the following question: was the Bandung Project workable? In other words, would it facilitate the effective establishment of modernized, national capitalist societies striving to catch up with the advanced societies within a framework of interdependence on the world scale? Or was it utopian, in the measure to which the objective sought would necessarily have required a radicalization of the Project that would shift it beyond the capitalist logic that inspired it? Some asserted that the national bourgeoisie still had a historic mission to fulfil, while others argued that this was an illusion doomed to end in rapid disillusionment. I was of the latter school, and I think history has proved us right.

So the time has come to define the challenges afresh, on the basis of achievements chalked up during the so-called 'development decades', while taking due account of the new configuration of the global system.

A New Agenda: Analysing the Diversity of the Third World and Reconstructing the Social Power of the Popular Classes

I propose, then, to analyse the diversity of what used to be called the Third World, using the competitive capacity of the various partners in the system as a basic criterion. On this basis, the peripheral societies fall into two distinct categories: on the one hand there are those whose manufactured products have achieved a competitive edge on the world market; on the other, there are those societies which, either because they have still not entered the industrial age, or because their industries are still far from achieving a competitive potential, remain trapped in the role of exporters of raw materials, prisoners of an outmoded division of labour.

The first group comprises the countries of East Asia, Latin America, and, to a lesser extent, India and South-East Asia. In the jargon of development managers, these are the real 'developing countries', meaning that they are seriously engaged in catching up with the developed societies. In my opinion, they constitute the real periphery of the emerging world system. The pattern of their industrialization resembles a gigantic sub-contracting enterprise controlled from countries at the centre of the system and working through what I call the five new monopolies (see pp. 3–5), which enable the latter to polarize the world for their exclusive benefit.

The second group (comprising all Africa, including North Africa and South Africa), sometimes referred to as the Fourth World, faces the prospect of further marginalization in the new world order.

The various ideologies and strategies proffered by ruling regimes are the means they use in their endeavour to manage the crisis of the emergent system. Their management style leans heavily on a patchwork of rhetoric gleaned from disparate sources, haphazardly buttressed with arguments of varying degrees of validity, most of them presenting a moral veneer, all recycled in the service of the existing regime. For example, in the name of the construction of a world system, and of the inadequacy of the outmoded concept of the nation, attempts are made to justify the diktat that now uses the UN flag as a flimsy fig leaf while beating down the states on the system's periphery into down-and-out entities incapable of resisting the worldwide onslaught of the market. And for this purpose such causes as the defence of minority rights are exploited. In the name of privatization, strenuous efforts are made to reinforce the efficiency of technological and financial monopolies, and to keep peripheral states defenceless in these domains. In the name of the environment, societies of the centre accuse peripheral states of waste, while themselves strengthening their monopoly over access to global resources and reaffirming their right to waste them. In the name of a manipulated democracy they arrogate to themselves the right to unlimited intervention.

It is the duty of the intelligentsia, especially those of the Third World and Africa, to deconstruct the new justificatory rhetoric, thus laying bare its functional connections with the tactical and strategic objectives of crisis management. We cannot, however, do this as long as we cling to time-worn formulae left in the dust by the renovated thrust of the world system. We need, therefore, here and now, to seize the progressive, democratic issues given a high profile because of the waning of postwar models, in order to give the attention and the thinking focused on them a radical spin.

Failing that, which is to say, if the intelligentsia flunks the test in these domains, the cycle of spontaneous and inadequate reactions from peoples crushed by the new worldwide polarization is bound to continue, and the energies generated will just as surely be harnessed by the dominant regimes in their determination to manage the crisis. I have in mind here the various centrifugal ethnic and communal forces, the nostalgic cultural revivalists, and especially the religious antiquarians active these days, whose devastating impact, notably in the disillusioned Fourth World, has taken on such tragic dimensions.

In the face of these crisis-management ideologies and strategies, the intelligentsia ought to respond with a positive contribution to the crystallization of alternative proposals offering real solutions to the crisis. I have no intention of proffering ready-made nostrums. Still, I think it useful to recapitulate a few basic concepts that could help reshape effective strategies for resolving the crisis while at the same time preparing the ground for a people's international, robust enough to deal effectively with the world-devouring appetite of capital. These suggestions would presuppose inputs from all levels, from the grassroots to states, regions and the world system as a whole.

Their implementation would require the creation, perhaps in gradual stages, of anti-comprador fronts in the peripheral societies, since comprador-based social alliances are precisely those that fit into the capitalist design for a new world order. It would also call for programmes aimed at the restructuring of states capable of meeting the challenge. For there is no way the five monopolies identified earlier can be broken without the creation, in a major regional environment, of an economic, political, cultural and military power strong enough to meet the challenge. The objectives of democratization linked with social advancement for the ordinary classes, of respect for ethnic, religious and other differences coupled with the promotion of freedom and diversity in these areas, could provide a starting point for such a necessary reconstruction. In Africa, it is time to breathe new life into the concepts of pan-Africanism and pan-Arabism, pushed off centre-stage by the earlier successes of the development process, now that the hollowness of those past successes is so clear.

Lastly, at the level of the world system, the struggle should aim at a reconstruction based on the negotiated creation of major regional blocs strong enough to meet current challenges. This reconstruction would of course cover the economic sphere: exchange connections and the definition of operational modalities for new monetary, financial, scientific, technological, commercial and environmental institutions designed to replace the World Bank, the International Monetary Fund, the General Agreement on Trade and Tariffs, the Agreement on Patents and Copyright, and so on. It would also be involved in political organization. For that reason there would have to be a renegotiation of the role of the UN, in a process that I see as a new multipolar strategy of delinking.

These proposals will no doubt be glibly dismissed as utopian. Utopian they certainly are, in the common understanding of the term, meaning that they look forward to changes to which current trends are not necessarily set to lead. In other words, the really existing social, political and ideological forces of the moment are not headed in the directions indicated. But there is a sense in which they are far from utopian: for the first steps in this direction would trigger off a virtuous cycle of changes snowballing into a major movement. In other words, the utopia under discussion here is a positive, creative one, and it has my wholehearted commitment. In any case, in the absence of such positive utopias, the peoples of the world invariably react to their desperate circumstances by reviving other types of utopia. Hence the surge of enthusiasm for fundamentalist religious movements. The difference is that those other utopias are dangerous, on account of their inherently backward orientations. Worse still, the religious utopias are ineffective in the sense that their basic culture-bound focus makes them perfectly compatible with a supine capitulation to the imperatives of the emerging capitalist world order as far as economic management is concerned.

The same critics who will dismiss my proposals as utopian will, as usual, keep intoning the refrain 'There Is No Alternative', now so predictable it has been encapsulated in an acronym, the TINA syndrome. We should combat this syndrome as absurd and criminal. In all situations there are alternatives. That is the very meaning of the concept of human freedom. It is rather amusing to see managerial types who dismiss Marxism, for example, as unduly deterministic, proffering this other vulgar, absolute kind of determinism. Moreover, the social design they seek to defend with this argument, namely the market-based management of the world system, is utopian in the worst sense of the term, a reactionary, criminal utopia, doomed in any case to fall apart under the pressure of its own highly explosive charge.

In the current state of the world, the intelligentsia faces a new set of daunting responsibilities. In previous phases of Africa's history, during the national liberation struggle, and later in the development decades, it fulfilled its mission quite honourably. In those days, institutions like IDEP, the Third World Forum and CODESRIA struggled side by side with numerous committed academics in lively intellectual encounters, making a rich and fruitful contribution to progressive forces. Admittedly, their work then was made easier by the fact that they could count on support from national liberation parties or from progressive forces making constructive contributions in the period after the retrieval of independence. In other words, they were backed by real, organized social and political forces. Unfortunately, there were times when such connections engendered dangerous illusions, leading to subsequent back-sliding.

We live now under a different configuration. The ruling classes, misnamed the élite, rationalize their collaboration with the scheme for the worldwide expansion of capitalism, which makes their peoples underdogs, in terms of 'Afro-pessimism', a set of negative attitudes they affect in common with the managerial functionaries of the world system. Cut adrift from these false élites, the ordinary classes try to cope as best they can, sometimes coming up with creative feats in their daily struggles for survival. Meanwhile the intelligentsia seems absent from the fray. It is high time it took back its rightful position.

Clearly, the crisis will not be resolved until popular, democratic forces capable of dominating the society get together again. But all effective hegemony depends on the presence of ideological and strategic instruments. In the creation of these tools the intelligentsia has a huge responsibility. It is its mission to establish bonds between its own productive thinking and the aspirations and actions of the popular classes, making them social partners; without this each is doomed to endure social isolation.

Needless to say, in this initial phase of reconstruction the relevant issue is not the immediate take-over of power. The first task ahead, instead, is the reconstruction of the social power of the popular classes, eroded by the ongoing crisis.

References

Amin, Samir, *Empire of Chaos,* Monthly Review Press, 1993
Amin, Samir, *Rereading the Post-War Period, an Intellectual Itinerary,* Monthly Review
   Press, New York, 1994

Index

aeronautics, US subsidies, 31
Afghanistan, 61
Africa: 'Afro-pessimism', 151;
balkanization, 89; Caribbean
Pacific Group (ACP), 117; Fourth
Worldization, 38; intelligensia,
147, 149, 152; pan-Africanism, 128,
150; polyglot, 62; sub-
Saharan, 88
Agreement on Patents and Copyright,
150
agriculture, 1, 114, 117; subsidies,
31; World Bank ideology, 25
Albania, 109
Algeria, 84
alienation, 140-1
Angola, 75
Arab world, 62, 117; pan-Arabism,
150; unity, 128
Arruda, Marcos, 14
Asia: 'Asia-Pacific Zone', 37; East,
70; South East, 51, 99-100
assimilationism, 84-5
Aswan Dam, 24
atlanticism, 93
Auschwitz, 137
Australia, 83
Austro-Hungarian Empire, 66, 86

Baghdad, 66
Balkans, the, 69
Bandung Project, 17, 23-4, 32-4, 46,
90, 93-4, 96, 101, 144, 147-8
banks, internationalization, 35-6
Baran, Paul, 19
Baudrillard, Jean, 136
Belguim, 129
Berbers, 62
Bismarck, Otto von, 51, 129

Blair House agreement, 30
Bolshevism, 87; revolution, 66
Brandt Report, 72
Brazil, 77, 100
Bretton Woods, 17-18, 20, 39, 47
Brezhnev, Leonid, 48
Britain, 66, 82, 115, 129; history, 83;
industry, 121;
the City, 120; the Commonwealth,
128
Bulgaria, 127
Bundesbank, the, 8, 53, 126
bureaucracies, private, 33

Canada, 52, 70, 119
capital: accumulation, 57; movements, 114; floating, 26
capitalism: classical, 1; historical
limit, 75; utopianism, 98;
wildcat, 8; 'without capitalists', 15,
17, 140
Casanova, P.G., 103
Central Intelligence Agency (CIA),
22
Chamber of Commerce, international,
30
chaos, 2, 6, 17, 102-3, 127, 132
Chiapas revolt, 38
China, 9, 52, 53, 68, 70-1, 87-8, 99-
100, 122; development, 10;
revolution, 94
cinema and TV production, 119
citizens, 81
Clinton, Bill, 14, 39, 48
Cote d'Ivoire, 25
Cold War, the, 94
colonialism, 63, 85, 119; massacres,
137
commercial law, 118
Common Agricultural Policy (CAP),
30, 114, 116-17
communism, 127; european parties,
112; nomenclature, 46;

Zed Titles on Globalization
Studies in International Political Economy

Nassau Adams: WORLDS APART:The North-South Divide and the International System

Samir Amin: CAPITALISM IN THE AGE OF GLOBALIZATION: The Management of Contemporary Society

Asoka Bandarage: WOMEN, POPULATION AND GLOBAL CRISIS: A Political-Economic Analysis

Ricardo Carrere and Larry Lohmann: PULPING THE SOUTH: Industrial Tree Plantations and the World Paper Economy

Michel Chossudovsky: THE GLOBALIZATION OF WORLD POVERTY: Impacts of IMF and World Bank Reforms

Gaffikin and Morrissey: THE NEW UNEMPLOYED: Joblessness and Poverty in the Market Economy

Bjorn Hettne et al: INTERNATIONAL POLITICAL ECONOMY: Understanding Global Disorder

Heyzer, Lycklama a Nijeholt, and Werekoon: THE TRADE IN DOMESTIC WORKERS: Causes, Mechanisms and Consequences of International Migration

Terence Hopkins and Immanuel Wallerstein et al: THE AGE OF TRANSITION: Trajectory of the World-System, 1945-2025

Brendan Martin: IN THE PUBLIC INTEREST? Privatization and Public Sector Reform

Lydia Potts: THE WORLD LABOUR MARKET: A History of Migration

Mihaly Simai (ed): GLOBAL EMPLOYMENT: An International Investigation into the Future of Work (2 volumes)

Henk Thomas (ed); GLOBALIZATION AND THIRD WORLD TRADE UNIONS